CROSSWORD PUZZLES

BOOST YOUR BRAINPOWER IN MINUTES

Publications International, Ltd.

Let's get social!
@Publications_International
@PublicationsInternational
@BrainGames.TM
www.pilbooks.com

GET CLUED IN!

Grab a pencil and get ready! The clues in these crossword puzzles touch on a variety of subjects, including movies, music, geography, and more. Don't worry if you get stuck. Answers are conveniently located at the back of the book for when you need a hint or have strained your brain enough.

The puzzles may be difficult, but there are many ways you can solve these challenges. First of all, always work in pencil, because you never know when an answer you're "pretty" sure about ends up not fitting into the greater scheme of the puzzle. Also, always try to solve the fill-in-the-blank clues first; they are generally an easy access point. You can try solving two- and three-letter, plural, and abbreviated clues first, too. These will hint at some of the longer, more difficult clues.

Happy puzzling!

COMFY AT HOME

ACROSS

1. Child in the care of a guardian
5. Bad sound for a balloonist
8. Axe handle
12. Antioxidant berry
13. Light brew, for short
14. "Bearded" flower
15. $20 bill dispensers
16. Disco-era kid
17. Dennis the Menace's friend
18. Relaxing wooden seat
21. Don Ho's instrument, informally
22. Fond du ___ (Wisconsin city)
23. A journalistic "W"
26. "___ Miserables" (Broadway musical)
27. Contents of jewel cases
30. Down-home wood burner
33. Emcee's aid
34. Cap, as on spending
35. Ancient Aegean land
36. Boxer's poke
37. "Dune" co-composer Brian
38. It makes for a cozy night's sleep
45. Get a new mortgage, informally
46. ___ room (place for air hockey)
47. Big party
48. It serves Jerusalem
49. Picasso's year
50. French river or department
51. Charlotte Bronte's "Jane ___"
52. Auctioneer's batch
53. Dental image

DOWN

1. WWII woman
2. Deeds, in Latin
3. Freeway entrance or exit
4. "Do not" follower, on a closed-door sign
5. Impish dust sprinkler
6. Be the first act
7. Dinner-plate garnish
8. Soprano's top note
9. "Carmen" song
10. Concluded, in Cannes
11. Old emperor of Russia
19. "___ and the Bee," 2006 film
20. Oleg of fashion
23. Keystrokes meas.
24. ___ polloi
25. "And so on" letters
26. Atty.'s degree
27. "Vaya ___ Dios"
28. 506, in old Rome
29. Sailor's realm
31. Politically left-leaning

32. Handyman's tote

36. 8-pointer in Scrabble

37. Disney World's ___ Center

38. At no cost to you

39. Difficult to grasp, as an elongated fish

40. A long way off

41. Mini-Vegas

42. Lion's den

43. Bones, anatomically

44. Curds and ___ (Muffet's meal)

1	2	3	4	■	5	6	7	■	8	9	10	11
12				■	13			■	14			
15				■	16			■	17			
18				19				20				
■	■	■	21			■	22			■	■	■
23	24	25			■	26			■	27	28	29
30					31				32			
33			■	34			■	35				
■	■	■	36			■	37			■	■	■
38	39	40				41				42	43	44
45				■	46			■	47			
48				■	49			■	50			
51				■	52			■	53			

Answers on page 172.

MAGICAL WORLD OF TEA

ACROSS

1. Feed for a fee, as cattle
5. Remove with teeth: 2 wds.
11. Moon goddess
12. Abbr. on a map
13. ___ Lingus, Irish carrier
14. Symbol of life
15. Japanese ceremonial beverage: 2 wds.
17. Secret agent's work
19. Genetic fingerprint
20. Scott ___, actor
22. Type of wave
26. Language spoken along the African coast
28. Coal deposit
30. Very long sentence
31. Publisher's employees, for short
32. Indian tea state
34. Mortgage ratio: abbr.
35. Small really badly
37. Vehicle shoe
38. ___ Messi, soccer star
39. Ponzi scheme, e.g.
41. Basketball dunk
43. Old PC platform: abbr.
45. Forever, old-style
48. Drink of soaked leaves
52. Origin
53. Padre ___, Italian friar canonized in 2002

54. Suffix with eloqu
55. "Hurry up!"
56. Burn slowly with no flame
57. African howler

DOWN

1. "Too bad"
2. Explosive source of theine
3. Pitch-black
4. Indian title
5. Calc. key
6. Pay attention to
7. Sports, e.g.
8. Cereal ingredient
9. Service charge
10. Italian monk
12. Most custardy
16. Execute perfecly
18. Astronaut's employer
21. Desert retreat
23. Pickle herb
24. Time for the siesta
25. Turning counterclockwise
26. Cut made by a saw
27. Away from port
29. ___ Dietrich, actress
33. Vegan's no-no
36. Spiral-horned cousin of caribou

40. Given medicine

42. Compassion

44. Trig functon

46. Where the Colosseum is

47. European active erupter

48. Internet addresses: abbr.

49. Matchsticks game

50. ___ Fighters, rock band

51. Text-reading tech.

1	2	3	4			5	6	7		8	9	10
11					12					13		
14					15			16				
17				18			19					
			20			21		22		23	24	25
26		27		28			29		30			
31				32				33		34		
35			36		37					38		
39				40		41			42			
			43		44		45			46		47
48	49	50				51			52			
53				54					55			
56								57				

Answers on page 172.

IN THE KITCHEN

ACROSS

1. Adroit exploit
5. Belief system, slangily
8. Bob or weave
12. Backscratcher target
13. "Read Across America" grp.
14. Adjective after "ye"
15. Contrary to Miss Manners
16. "What Not to Wear" network
17. Battle of Normandy city
18. Zapper at home
21. 6 on a phone
22. Lady of Spain, briefly
23. Beyond enthusiasm
26. '60s platters
27. Regret
30. Battery-operated or plug-in carver
33. Humorist's skill
34. Fire up, as an engine
35. Discontinued Apple laptop
36. Distinction, slangily
37. "CSI" specimen
38. Slicing-dicing appliance
45. "Damn Yankees" heroine
46. Any of les Antilles
47. "I can't carry a ___ in a bucket"
48. "SNL"'s Samberg
49. 90-degree bend
50. ___ nitrite (heart medicine)
51. "Not for me"
52. Abe's "The Godfather" role
53. ___ Music (Brian Eno's old band)

DOWN

1. Hard, as a mattress
2. Case for needles and pins
3. Band with a lightning bolt in its logo
4. Of heat
5. Bisected, say
6. "Gone Girl" actress Ward
7. Epic battle in technology
8. Beauty butter
9. Former King of Norway
10. Cannes brainstorm
11. Sherilyn of "Twin Peaks"
19. Vacationing, perhaps
20. "Tobacco Road" author Caldwell
23. Feline plaint
24. He perfected the rope-a-dope
25. "Nothing but ___!"
26. Daughter of Steven Tyler
27. Brazilian vacation spot, informally
28. "Close Encounters" sight
29. "Spider!"
31. Prepares Mexican beans
32. Jordan, for one

36. Decisive times

37. Boombox battery

38. Beat, as wings

39. Actress Chaplin of "Game of Thrones"

40. 88 or 98 automaker

41. Big pot of stew

42. Asian wrestling

43. Banded agate

44. Depend (on)

1	2	3	4		5	6	7		8	9	10	11
12					13				14			
15					16				17			
18				19				20				
			21				22					
23	24	25				26				27	28	29
30					31				32			
33				34				35				
			36				37					
38	39	40				41				42	43	44
45					46				47			
48					49				50			
51					52				53			

Answers on page 172.

FINISH THE ADAGE

ACROSS

1. After-school group
5. "Cakes and ___" (Maugham novel)
8. Didn't have to guess
12. Aesop character who lost a race
13. ___ Fail (Irish "Stone of Destiny")
14. Actress Petty of "Orange Is the New Black"
15. One in agreement
17. "Bearded" flower
18. Practice . . . (finish the adage)
20. Fleur de ___
21. Big palooka
22. Chick of jazz
25. Au ___ (in gravy)
26. Big name in casual clothes
29. Good fences make…(finish the adage)
32. Charged-up particle
33. Airline to Amsterdam
34. Breakwater
35. "Get it?"
36. "How delightful!"
37. A watched . . . (finish the adage)
44. Peru's capital
45. Invites for a visit
46. Colorado Springs Acad.
47. "___-Pan" (Clavell novel)
48. Air outlet
49. Diner's list
50. German "one"
51. It is, in Spain

DOWN

1. Ballplayer's cheekful
2. Eye protector
3. "Major" constellation
4. Describing a brow
5. Glee club voices
6. "In ___ of flowers . . . "
7. One of a swimmer's pair
8. Film studio light
9. "The Thin Man" role
10. "Spamalot" creator Idle
11. Coin-in-the-fountain thought
16. Joltin' Joe, e.g.
19. They have to be done fast
22. 3-D graphics in movies
23. Tic-tac-toe win
24. Harry Potter's pal Weasley
25. Carrey or Belushi
26. "You've ___ Mail"
27. It's often left hanging
28. "Gangnam Style" rapper
30. Kick up a notch
31. Make sense for
35. Military slang for a muddled mess

36. Big name in pest control

37. "Clue" professor

38. River from Belgium to France

39. Fraud-fighting Fed

40. Morales of "Bad Boys"

41. "Blue Tail Fly" singer Burl

42. Fasting period

43. Latina lass: Abbr.

1	2	3	4		5	6	7		8	9	10	11
12					13				14			
15				16					17			
18								19				
			20				21					
22	23	24				25				26	27	28
29					30				31			
32				33				34				
			35				36					
37	38	39				40				41	42	43
44					45							
46					47				48			
49					50				51			

Answers on page 172.

AMERICAN FOLK TALES

ACROSS

1. Balkan native
5. A helping hand
8. Any of the Galapagos
12. Base of Hawaiian poi
13. Card game based on crazy eights
14. "Mister Roberts" setting
15. "Amo, amas, ___"
16. Shudder-inducing
18. Paul Bunyan's awesome bovine companion
20. "Fiddlesticks!"
21. "Do the Right Thing" director Spike
22. Ham's device
25. Bk. before Numbers
26. Badly lit
29. Niagara Falls legend about a young Indian woman
32. "Sister Act" sister
33. Gave dinner to
34. Big name in cameras
35. "One Day ___ Time"
36. Not hers or his
37. Legendary logger and Forest Service warden
44. As a lark
45. Any NATO member to another
46. Belfry sound
47. Athlete's outfit
48. Buck or ram
49. Girl in a Salinger story
50. Actress Thompson in "Back to the Future"
51. Coup d'___ (uprising)

DOWN

1. Blind guess
2. The genus that contains alpacas
3. Baghdad native
4. Poll worker's request
5. Anything whatever
6. About, in legal memos
7. There's one in "fishhook"
8. Debatable topic
9. Brake pad
10. Prom ride, for short
11. Climber's goal
17. Near-final hour
19. More frequently than is good
22. Watergate monogram
23. Nonprofessional sports org.
24. Annoying racket
25. Inc., in England
26. Hagar's creator Browne
27. Equal: Prefix
28. Peak, for short
30. Scared
31. Title incorrectly

35. Deft and active

36. Old Greek region

37. Mock

38. French islands

39. Bowie's rock genre

40. Bride's month

41. Bedframe part

42. Ceramic jug

43. Bolshevik's denial

Answers on page 173.

TO KILL A MOCKINGBIRD

ACROSS

1. "To Kill a Mockingbird"'s state
8. Ancient Greek gathering place
13. Oil and ___
14. Painter of cafe scenes
15. "College" member who votes for president
16. ___ once (suddenly)
17. "___ Lama Ding Dong" ('60s tune)
18. Golda Meir was one
20. "Mockingbird" girl and narrator
22. "Mockingbird" character Radley
23. Control-tower employee: Abbr.
24. As of yet
26. Coin of little worth
27. "The Great" czar
30. Gravelly ridges
33. 1921 man-vs.-robot play
34. "Grey's Anatomy" role
36. A pitching ace has a low one, in brief
37. Outer: Prefix
38. Once ___ (annually)
42. Asked someone to "hush"
44. Mechanical click
45. Go for ___ (take the car out)
46. Like wanted criminals
49. Cotton thread used for gloves
50. Christmas tree shedding
51. Asian coins or weights
52. Goldilocks's pride

DOWN

1. Affirms with confidence
2. Delicate purple
3. Prefix meaning "wind"
4. "___ I said so!"
5. 15-percenter: Abbr.
6. "Little Red Book" chairman
7. Exuberant Spanish cry
8. Ruben ___, Phillies Gold Glove-winning shortstop
9. Big, fancy dinner
10. How some cars are acquired
11. House broker
12. Gregory's role in "Mockingbird"
19. More achy
21. Craggy hill
25. Atticus, Scout and Jem's last name
27. Make ready for a winter storm, as a highway
28. Continent-spanning landmass
29. Roam (about)
31. Assigner of nine-digit nos.
32. Data-input devices
35. Former Secretary General of the U.N.
37. Anglo-Saxon serfs

39. British nobles

40. "Oh, shucks!"

41. Like May-to-August months

43. Best friend of Jem and Scout in "Mockingbird"

47. Dutch artist Gerard ___ Borch

48. "Mockingbird" author Harper ___

1	2	3	4	5	6	7		8	9	10	11	12
13								14				
15								16				
17						18	19					
20				21		22				23		
			24		25					26		
27	28	29					30	31	32			
33					34	35						
36				37				38		39	40	41
42			43						44			
45						46	47	48				
49						50						
51						52						

Answers on page 173.

POP STARS

ACROSS

1. Little white lies
5. Improv routine
8. Allied jumping-off point of July 1944
12. Dust Bowl state: Abbr.
13. Big fuss
14. Aid for catching a mouse
15. Film critic
17. Bee, to Opie
18. Fred Astaire title role
20. "For ___ a jolly good fellow..."
21. "All's well," in space
22. Artifact from the past
25. African despot Amin
26. Play ___ with (make trouble for)
29. Apply frosting
30. Barbecue chef's wear
32. Track's governing org.
33. Baby's word
34. Gp. that sticks to their guns
35. Aisle with butter and eggs
37. Courtroom oath
38. Bygone nuclear agcy.
39. Little Orphan Annie's guardian
46. Berry plugged as a superfood
47. No-no at some intersections
48. "As I see it," online
49. ___ long (poetic "soon")
50. Assam silkworm
51. "Cheep" accommodations?
52. Angler's pole
53. Plaintiff's opposite: Abbr.

DOWN

1. Country legend Tennessee Ernie
2. Assemble-it-yourself furniture seller
3. Wide rd.
4. Gave an informal greeting
5. Cries loudly
6. Prefix for graph or logical
7. "The Wizard of Oz" weather event
8. Celery stem
9. "Can't argue with that"
10. "Auld ___ Syne"
11. Makes a choice
16. Head turner, say
19. Spend more than you have
22. Fix, as a horse race
23. "Green" opener
24. Author Tolstoy
25. "Deathtrap" author Levin
26. Yes, in Yokohama
27. Blade in the water
28. Act like a bull?
31. Sneak who's up to no good
36. More keen

37. "It is a tale told by an ___"
38. Barked, Sandy-style
39. Hammett's "The ___ Curse"
40. As high as you can go
41. Dashes in a code

42. Dynamic start?
43. Fix for what ails you
44. Actor-singer Kristofferson
45. Bean or dragon

1	2	3	4		5	6	7		8	9	10	11
12					13				14			
15				16					17			
18							19					
			20				21					
22	23	24				25				26	27	28
29				30	31					32		
33				34				35	36			
			37				38					
39	40	41				42				43	44	45
46					47							
48					49				50			
51					52				53			

Answers on page 173.

LOOK ON THE BRIGHT SIDE

ACROSS

1. "Man, that's a relief!"
5. Subject of a 1773 protest
8. Boat ramp
12. "Drat!" is a mild one
13. Belief system
14. Bit of deception
15. "Cubist" Rubik
16. "7 Faces of Dr. ___" (Tony Randall pic)
17. Capital near fjords
18. Scintillating
21. Perfect to a gymnast
22. "Funeral in Berlin" author Deighton
23. Angry growl
25. It's not much
28. "Knot" homophone
30. Canada's neighbor, colloquially
33. Bogus
35. Letters in a URL
37. Boardroom attire
38. Instrument for the musically inept, maybe
40. "Mighty" tree
42. "Now do you believe me?"
43. Abysmal score
45. Actress Ullmann or Tyler
47. Campaigner, for short
49. Shining intensely

54. Disney's boy detective
56. Copy
57. "Parlez-___ francais?"
58. "Citizen ___" (Welles film)
59. Catnip mouse, for a cat
60. "___ Dinka Doo" (Jimmy Durante song)
61. "Cogito, ___ sum"
62. Language ending, sometimes
63. "Home on the Range" critter

DOWN

1. Bellyacher's litany
2. Dwell on tediously
3. 11,000-foot Italian peak
4. Fingerprint feature
5. To this moment
6. "NYPD Blue" star Morales
7. First ___ equals
8. "No more seats" sign
9. Gleaming
10. "Lord of the Flies" setting
11. Feudal drudge
19. "Jeopardy!" whiz Jennings
20. African antelope
24. Balaam's beast
25. Informal reproach
26. "Eureka!"
27. Eye-popping

29. Deuce

31. 'Bah!' relative

32. Absorbed the loss of

34. A brother of Curly

36. Large freshwater sport fish

39. Any planet, to a bard

41. About 5/8 of a mi.

44. Speechify

46. Intensely graphic

47. Chinese dog, for short

48. Rubaiyat maker

50. Nasdaq debuts

51. Tip-top

52. Cook in the microwave, slangily

53. Former Russian emperor

55. "The Lip" of baseball

1	2	3	4		5	6	7		8	9	10	11
12					13				14			
15					16				17			
18				19				20		21		
			22				23		24			
25	26	27		28		29		30			31	32
33			34		35		36		37			
38			39		40		41		42			
		43			44		45		46			
47	48			49		50				51	52	53
54			55		56				57			
58					59				60			
61					62				63			

Answers on page 173.

IT'S IN YOUR HANDS

ACROSS

1. It's in your hands
5. Ice cream flavor, briefly
9. Audible dance
12. At leisure
13. Carrie on "The King of Queens"
14. A hot time, in Paris
15. Break ground
16. Lhasa ___
17. Coastal eagle
18. Man with a couch
20. Become frantic
22. Koop and Elders, for short
23. ___-Locka (town near Miami)
24. "Star Wars" genre
25. Having color
26. Immune system component
27. Patrick Stewart role
30. British bishops' hats
31. Time and ___ (overtime pay)
32. Saloon sounds
33. Polynesian wraparound skirt
34. Kind of battery: Abbr.
35. Relative of mdse.
38. Big occasion
39. Handel opus
41. Big foot spec
42. West Point initials
44. "The ___ Reader": eclectic magazine
45. French rifle range
46. "Walkabout" director Nicolas
47. "___ and the Detectives" (old Disney film)
48. "Roswell" regulars
49. Aer Lingus land
50. It's in your hands

DOWN

1. ___ a fiddle
2. Going too far, in a way
3. Earthen jars
4. "The Farmer in the ___"
5. Held tightly
6. Group of seven
7. Economic gp. formed in Bogota, 1948
8. They're in your hands
9. More microscopic
10. Not much at all
11. They're in your hands
19. It's in your hands
21. The FDIC may insure them
25. Guitarist Eddie Van ___
27. Tahiti's capital
28. "Here's the solution!"
29. They're in your hands
30. Odometer marking

32. It's in your hands

35. Cuban military base, for short

36. Zebra ___ (aquarium fish)

37. Beach find

40. Bird feeder cake

43. "___ sez to the guy..."

1	2	3	4		5	6	7	8		9	10	11
12					13					14		
15					16					17		
18				19				20	21			
22				23				24				
			25					26				
27	28	29					30					
31						32						
33					34				35	36	37	
38					39			40				
41				42	43				44			
45				46					47			
48				49					50			

Answers on page 174.

THAT'S A NO-NO

ACROSS

1. Sailors
5. Frequently, in verse
8. Medal recipient
12. Away from shore
13. Kiboshed
15. Influence unfairly
16. Santana's first hit, 1970
17. "In all probability . . ."
19. Alternative to nothing
20. 20-vol. lexicon
21. Actor ____ Elba of "The Wire"
23. Start of Mr. Rogers' song
26. Creator of lofty lines
27. Foster, as wrongdoing
28. Disallowed
31. Not permitted
33. "Peter and the Wolf" duck
34. Chemically inactive
36. Abdomen, in slang
37. Instructional sequence
38. Couple in Cancun
41. 1958-1961 alliance
43. Fairies and pixies, e.g.
45. Napoleonic leader?
48. "Nasty" first name in tennis
49. Not legal
50. "Hello, Dolly!" lead role
51. Part of Ali's record
52. Fleur de ____
53. First place?

DOWN

1. Prohibited
2. Line to the audience
3. Check the total of
4. Attitude
5. Went too far
6. High temperatures
7. Angle or cycle starter
8. Allen Ginsberg beat poem
9. And elsewhere: Lat.
10. "Star Wars: The Force Awakens" girl
11. Carry-____ (airplane totes)
14. "Gil ____" (Le Sage novel)
18. Assistant on the Hill
22. "Definitely maybe"
24. A golfer puts it in the ground
25. Benchmark, briefly
26. Bill below five
27. "Guest" at certain meals
28. Cranberry "field"
29. "Aladdin" monkey
30. Unfit for
32. British Isles tongue
35. Anthony who sang "What Kind of Fool Am I"

37. Mlle. from Acapulco

38. Distributed bit by bit

39. "Drab" army color

40. Ball of yarn

42. Feels a bit punk

44. Dossier

45. Army sleeper

46. Arctic diver

47. Belt hole maker

1	2	3	4		5	6	7		8	9	10	11
12					13			14				
15					16							
17				18				19				
20				21			22			23	24	25
			26						27			
28	29	30					31	32				
33					34	35						
36				37						38	39	40
		41	42			43			44			
45	46				47				48			
49									50			
51					52				53			

Answers on page 174.

BADDIES OF FICTION

ACROSS

1. Hot rocks
5. Boggy land
8. Belch, say
12. "Deliver us from ___"
13. "Do the Right Thing" director
14. Hip-hop trio Salt-N-___
15. Count calories
16. Archer's wood
17. Arrogant sort
18. "The Demon Barber of Fleet Street"
21. 1985 Kurosawa classic
22. A in German class?
23. Coal worker
26. "The Big Bang Theory" character from India
27. Barrel at a bash
30. "Nightmare on Elm Street" villain
33. It's often left hanging
34. A pal of Pooh
35. Easy gait
36. Big embrace
37. "Fifth Beatle" Yoko
38. "Psycho" weirdo
43. Sonny or Chastity
44. "___ culpa"
45. "Don't worry about me"
47. Orders a dog to attack
48. Escort's offering
49. 1980s Dodge model
50. "Iliad" war god
51. "___ Skylark" (Shelley)
52. Apollo acronym

DOWN

1. Blazed a trail
2. Alamo alternative
3. Panoramic sight
4. Did a tailoring job
5. Robin Hood portrayer Errol
6. Bigfoot's shoe size?
7. It begins in January
8. Big name in printers
9. Fix, as socks
10. It can help you carry a tune
11. Eatery check
19. Body part that vibrates
20. Baja border city
23. Artist's degree
24. Abbr. on a clothing reject tag
25. Hoop hanger
26. "King Kong" and "Citizen Kane" studio
27. C.I.A.'s Soviet counterpart
28. Aquarium wriggler
29. College sr.'s exam
31. Something to meditate on

32. Feeling

36. 1990s candidate ____ Perot

37. 2009 Peace Prize Nobelist

38. "Film ____ "(dark movie genre)

39. "The Raven" start

40. "Fiddling" emperor

41. Madame Bovary

42. Heirs, often

43. "Be prepared" org.

46. Cadenza maker

1	2	3	4		5	6	7		8	9	10	11
12					13				14			
15					16				17			
	18			19				20				
		21				22						
23	24	25				26				27	28	29
30					31				32			
33				34				35				
		36				37						
	38	39				40				41	42	
43					44				45			46
47					48				49			
50					51				52			

Answers on page 174.

WHAT'S COOKING

ACROSS

1. "Geek Squad" worker
5. "Indent" key
8. Airport boarding place
12. Salvation ___ (where many NFL players volunteer)
13. DVD predecessor
14. "Green" emotion
15. Disquiet
17. Alaskan Gold Rush town
18. "My Big Fat Greek Wedding" star Vardalos
19. ___ populi (popular opinion)
21. Breakfast order
28. It comes before "di-dah"
29. "Do Ya" rock band
30. Actor Flynn with a sword
31. Eye part with color
33. Catch-all term
35. "Buona ___" (Italian "Good evening")
36. Bedtime for many
38. Bath fixture
40. Chi. Clock setting
41. Musical toys
44. First lady
45. "Madama Butterfly" sash
46. Empty expanse
49. Pupil's writing need
54. Bali or Capri
55. Equals, in math
56. About in legalspeak
57. Blacken lightly
58. Denial from de Gaulle
59. Not at port

DOWN

1. Ancient cross
2. Coastal eagle
3. Meas. on IKEA boxes
4. "Laughing" critter
5. Stand for an idiot box
6. Athletes often tear it
7. Alla ___ (music notation)
8. Boomers' kids
9. "Feliz ___ Nuevo!" ("Happy New Year!")
10. "I really appreciate that," while texting
11. One of two that view
16. "Newsweek" rival
20. Poem that honors
21. Capri pants features
22. 1970's batting champ Rod
23. "Watch on the ___," 1941 Lillian Hellman play
24. Big-win, high-odds game
25. El ___ (Spanish artist)
26. Growth on English moors
27. Bed frame strips

32. Driver doing 90, say

34. Use a scalpel on

37. Network that aired "Jersey Shore"

39. Crib occupant

42. Georgia pie nut

43. Bone below the knee

46. "___ for Vengeance" (Grafton novel)

47. Ending for "verb" or "malt"

48. Dock workers' union

50. "___ y Plata" (Montana motto)

51. Appliance buttons

52. Portland's st.

53. Hawaii's Mauna ___

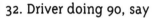

1	2	3	4		5	6	7		8	9	10	11
12					13				14			
15				16					17			
			18				19	20				
21	22	23				24				25	26	27
28				29				30				
31			32		33		34		35			
36				37		38		39		40		
41					42				43			
			44				45					
46	47	48			49	50				51	52	53
54					55				56			
57					58				59			

Answers on page 174.

STRICTLY PC

ACROSS

1. Dust bunny particle
5. Athos, to Aramis
8. Class exam
12. Attempt to persuade
13. Common soccer score
14. "... lamp ___ my feet": Psalms
15. Strict, restaurant-owning Seinfeld character
17. Arctic Blast maker
18. Lord's Prayer opener
19. Enjoyed takeout
21. Popular appetizer
28. First to leave a sinking ship?
29. Blackhawks and Red Wings org.
30. "An ___ of prevention..."
31. Ball-shaped cheese
33. So far
35. Angler's tangle
36. Did some rowing
38. Academic climber
40. Its cap. is Buenos Aires
41. Eldest son of Queen Elizabeth II
44. Anatomical eggs
45. "Bravo!"
46. "Ho-hum!"
49. Aromatic spice
54. Demon's doings
55. "Boy king" of Egypt
56. "Survivor" setting, often
57. Hard to make out
58. That man's
59. Former Soviet news agency

DOWN

1. Banquet hosts
2. Tic-tac-toe win, maybe
3. Cross-shaped Greek letter
4. John McCain, notably
5. Emma Goldman's goal
6. "Les ___" (eight-Tony winner)
7. "Sacro" attachment
8. Period of inactivity
9. Chapel Hill campus, for short
10. Suffix with Manhattan or Israel
11. "Sesame Street" Muppet in a tutu
16. "Cats" director Trevor ___
20. Bout ender, briefly
21. Before surgery, briefly
22. "M*A*S*H" corporal O'Reilly
23. "Pong" company
24. Acid used in soap
25. Old-style yearly record
26. Compassionate comment
27. Hanes competitor
32. Stag

34. Trebek and Sajak, e.g.

37. 605, to Cicero

39. "Boola Boola" school

42. "The Blue Marble" subject

43. Mail a payment

46. Mumbled assent

47. The second Mrs. Sinatra

48. "The ___" (Munchkinland musical)

50. French agreement

51. Botanist Gray

52. "Treasure Island" author monogram

53. Proposal response, often

1	2	3	4		5	6	7		8	9	10	11
12					13				14			
15				16					17			
			18				19	20				
21	22	23				24				25	26	27
28				29				30				
31			32		33		34		35			
36				37		38		39		40		
41					42				43			
			44				45					
46	47	48			49	50				51	52	53
54					55				56			
57					58				59			

Answers on page 175.

HORSE OPERAS

ACROSS

1. Arabian gulf
5. "American ___" (1999 Jason Biggs movie)
8. Architect's design
12. Sioux shelter: Var.
13. Gen.'s counterpart
14. Filigreed
15. On a liner, say
16. Tiny, to Angus
17. About, in contracts
18. 1949 western starring Clayton Moore and Jay Silverheels
21. Cries of discomfort
22. Kind or sort
23. Baseball Hall-of-Famer Tony
26. It's west of Afr.
27. Area for critical patients, briefly
30. 1950s western starring Gregory Peck
33. Alley-___ (basketball play)
34. Beloved animal
35. Grainy, maybe
36. Judge Lance ___ (1995 name in the news)
37. Anderson Cooper's channel
38. 1950 western with James Ellison and Julie Adams
45. "… softly and carry ___ stick"
46. "Texas Tea"
47. Bobber in a harbor
48. Rwanda native
49. It may be heard before a reception
50. Raggedy ___ (some dolls)
51. "Saving Private Ryan" event
52. A pocketful, in rhyme
53. Bee ___ ("Stayin' Alive" group)

DOWN

1. Rat ___ (gun sounds)
2. Act the gossip
3. Fencing weapon
4. "Soul Food" actress
5. Chessboard sixteen
6. Brainstorm, in Paris
7. Honored faculty retirees
8. Shoot at, as bottles on a fence
9. Lana of Smallville
10. Part of an estate
11. Manhattanite, for short
19. Admit
20. Little kid's words after cleaning his plate
23. '60s Pontiac muscle car
24. First of a journalist's five W's
25. Backwoods affirmative
26. At the back of a boat
27. "Addams Family" cousin
28. So-so mark, in school

29. Catering hall vessel

31. Modern film genre with dark themes

32. Purse

36. PC troubleshooter around the office

37. Actress Sevigny

38. Former Saudi king

39. "Nothing beats ___" (old beer slogan)

40. "Come in and ___ spell"

41. In apple-pie order

42. Ancient Germanic character

43. "How steak is done" sauce

44. "Swiss Family Robinson" author Johann

1	2	3	4		5	6	7		8	9	10	11
12					13				14			
15					16				17			
18			19				20					
			21				22					
23	24	25				26			27	28	29	
30				31				32				
33				34			35					
			36				37					
38	39	40			41				42	43	44	
45				46				47				
48				49				50				
51				52				53				

Answers on page 175.

HIT SONGS

ACROSS

1. Archery expert in legend
5. Commencement grp.
8. Not busy at all
12. A member of the Siouan people
13. Atomic particle
14. 1997 Prizms, e.g.
15. Malek of "Mr. Robot"
16. A HR produces at least one
17. Arctic reindeer herder
18. Song covered by the Beatles, 1963
21. Decorative coffee server
22. Also
23. Bacteriologist's dish
26. "Unagi" at the sushi bar
27. Cumberland, for one
30. Rock and roll standard covered by Fats Domino, 1956
33. Dreamworks ___ (movie studio)
34. Blade in the lake
35. Not boyish
36. Guggenheim Museum display
37. A caddy carries it
38. Elvis Presley's best-selling single, 1960
45. Jail for a sailor
46. A pitcher wants a low one, for short
47. Ancient Mariner's poem
48. Actress Skye of "Say Anything"
49. A stereotypical pirate may have one
50. Adult program rating
51. Court figure
52. Journal
53. Once around the sun

DOWN

1. Synagogue scroll
2. Coup d'___ (rebellion)
3. Mesa's cousin
4. Off-duty time
5. Ambulance alarm
6. Cop or call prefix
7. Brandy goblet
8. Alaskan white house
9. Academic official
10. Canter leisurely
11. Catch sight of
19. ___ Bridge (former name of New York's R.F.K. Bridge)
20. Lama, for one
23. "Nova" network
24. Grand Teton grazer
25. Harbor craft
26. Goof up
27. Card-player's cry
28. Partner of one?
29. Carry on, as a trade

31. Have nutritious foods
32. Julie of "Airplane!"
36. Hot temper
37. Fort ___ (North Carolina base)
38. Bird sacred to ancient Egyptians
39. Slacks, briefly

40. Angle ratio
41. "Milk's Favorite Cookie"
42. On the qui ___ (watchful)
43. "Clueless" was a retelling of it
44. Bottom or back

1	2	3	4	■	5	6	7	■	8	9	10	11
12				■	13			■	14			
15				■	16			■	17			
18			19				20					
■	■		21			■	22			■	■	■
23	24	25			■	26			■	27	28	29
30					31				32			
33			■	34			■	35				
■	■		36				■	37			■	■
38	39	40				41				42	43	44
45				■	46			■	47			
48				■	49			■	50			
51				■	52			■	53			

Answers on page 175.

CHARACTERS WE LOVE

ACROSS

1. On ___ (as a gamble)
5. Hogwarts mail carriers
9. Blocked from view
12. Cantina munchie
13. "Here comes trouble"
14. Academic URL ender
15. "Once ___ a time..."
16. Modern recording option
17. Abbr. after many a general's name
18. Teen sleuth of books, movies, TV
20. "Merry" month
21. A place to go in London?
22. "Sorry Not Sorry" singer Lovato
24. Bayou cuisine
27. Exhaust
30. Short nail
31. Take a load off
32. Aardvark's dinner
33. Africa's westernmost nation
35. Behave furtively
36. Ball-shaped cheese
37. Big name in averages
38. Award bestowed by the queen, for short
40. Legendary archer-bandit of English folklore
45. Fork out

46. State decisively
47. "Python" Eric
48. Make a mistake
49. Bloods or Crips
50. Cut of pork
51. Born as, for women
52. Art Deco artist
53. A.k.a. Cupid

DOWN

1. Astonish
2. Bear in the big chair
3. "The dismal science," briefly
4. Decided by reasoning
5. Perform better than
6. Electric-fan sound
7. Brief rave review
8. "Psycho" scene setting
9. Friend of Harry and Ron
10. Brainstormer's spark
11. Customs fee
19. "Round ___ virgin..."
23. "___, back on the farm..."
24. "60 Minutes" network
25. Is plural?
26. Bronte heroine
27. "Shop ___ you drop"
28. Acting guru Hagen

34

29. Cluck of disapproval

31. Russian tea urn

34. Grease monkey's workplace

35. Junior, to Senior

37. Funeral music

38. Transparent

39. Like Mother Hubbard's cupboard

41. Like a proposer's knee

42. Annoying smell

43. A little of this and a little of that

44. Bear lairs

1	2	3	4		5	6	7	8		9	10	11
12					13					14		
15					16					17		
18				19						20		
			21				22		23			
24	25	26				27					28	29
30					31				32			
33				34				35				
		36					37					
38	39			40		41				42	43	44
45				46					47			
48				49					50			
51				52					53			

Answers on page 175.

HOLDING HANDS

ACROSS

1. Give for free, slangily
5. Caught in the rain
8. Bigger than big
12. Fiery gemstone
13. 1040 org.
14. About which the Earth turns
15. Abominable Snowman
16. Golf ball placement
17. Boring method to learn by
18. Fancy light fixtures holding a hand?
21. Busy buzzer
22. A doctrine or theory
23. Young turkey
26. Bout stoppers, briefly
27. Mom's month
30. Control, as lions
31. Activated, as a fuse
32. Apple throwaway
33. Jean of Dada
34. Classic name for a dinosaur
35. "Every ___ Way But Loose" (1978 film)
36. "Groovy!" relative
37. Amazement
38. Like drip-dry garments, holding a hand?
43. Add a bit of color to
44. "The Hunt for ___ October"
45. Duel provoker

47. A cappella range
48. Mine material
49. Architect Saarinen
50. Baby chick's sound
51. "Yes" gesture
52. Flow slowly

DOWN

1. Affectedly shy
2. 11-member cartel
3. Calculus, for example
4. Easily shaped
5. "The Importance of Being Earnest" author
6. One of the five Great Lakes
7. "Cats" poet
8. "Scheherezade" setting
9. Caesar's wife
10. Beats it, in the backwoods
11. Compass point opposite WSW
19. Butterfly catcher
20. Orbiting lab, for short
23. Sch. booster group
24. Rowboat need
25. Ballgame official
26. "Kid-tested, mother-approved" cereal
27. "Me?" to Miss Piggy
28. Rainbow path

29. "Uh-huh"

31. Classic Chrysler model

32. Brie and gouda

34. Cheer shout

35. Internet letters

36. Camera lens setting

37. Came up with a sum

38. Craftiness

39. A chip in the pot, perhaps

40. "Quo Vadis?" emperor

41. Safe, at sea

42. Like some stamps or steaks

43. "This Is Spinal ___"

46. Football coach Warner

Answers on page 176.

GUESS THE THEME

ACROSS

1. "Hey!" on the road
5. "Dombey and ___" (Dickens novel)
8. Amateur
12. All-purpose trucks
13. Brain of a PC
14. Basketball need
15. "Contrary" girl of rhyme
16. Ben-Hur was chained to one for three years
17. Hand-knotted rugs
18. Prevent entrance, in a way
21. Enjoying a win streak
22. Churchyard tree in "Romeo and Juliet"
23. Outdoor lounging spot
26. Many a hand sanitizer
27. "Death Becomes ___" (Meryl Streep film)
30. Shareholder's payment
33. Baby sitter's handful
34. Type of jet engine
35. Goes to the polls
36. "Slippery" fish
37. "___ lords a-leaping"
38. Hurdy-gurdy
43. Big cat of the Americas
44. Acorn source
45. Burglar's haul
47. Cupid counterpart
48. National monogram
49. Breaks up
50. Au pair's charge
51. "Honor ___ father"
52. Drip through an opening

DOWN

1. Borrow (forever)
2. "And a lot of others besides that," in four letters
3. Dulles designer Saarinen
4. Like a mind reader
5. "Patton" portrayer
6. Bright-colored fish
7. Dance great Rudolf
8. Kind of pillow or rug
9. Cello player Ma
10. "The Lion King" sound effect
11. Black ___ (covert doings)
19. More flaky
20. Bring to one's door, as mail
23. Air pressure letters
24. Bank convenience, for short
25. "___ Chef"
26. Card game or drink
27. All ___ up (agitated)
28. 180 degrees from WSW
29. Blvd. crossers

31. Distribute sparingly

32. Computer attachments

36. Do blackboard duty

37. Sweet Hungarian wine

38. Cover up

39. Crazed way to run

40. Batted body part, briefly

41. Top notch

42. Bump on a log, say

43. Dino, for the Flintstones

46. A bit more than a pinch: Abbr.

1	2	3	4		5	6	7		8	9	10	11
12					13				14			
15					16				17			
	18			19				20				
			21				22					
23	24	25				26				27	28	29
30					31				32			
33				34				35				
			36				37					
	38	39				40				41	42	
43					44				45			46
47					48				49			
50					51				52			

Answers on page 176.

FUN FADS

ACROSS

1. Part of FWIW
4. Corn eater's discards
8. Citrus drinks
12. Fifties fad involving undulation
14. Denim king Strauss
15. Heading uphill or downhill, e.g.
16. "Israel Through My Eyes" author
17. Backyard barbecue spot
18. Faddish '70s toy that came in a box with air holes
20. Bygone nuclear agcy.
22. "All By Myself" singer Celine
23. Boss of Hazzard County
26. Assists
28. Be in poor health
31. Poi base
32. "L'il ol' me?"
33. Be in accord with
34. Calypso offshoot
35. Capital of Western Samoa
36. Octopus octet
37. Action word
39. Barrister's field
41. Watch-Me-Grow fad
44. "Animal House" getups
48. Child's punishment, maybe
49. Legal escape hatch
51. Bonnie hillside
52. Trippy fad light of the '60s
53. "Mama" ___ Elliot
54. Paparazzi target
55. Amphibious carrier, for short

DOWN

1. "Rooty Tooty Fresh and Fruity" restaurant
2. Albacore or bluefin
3. Bedframe strip
4. Actress Sevigny
5. "Tic Tac Dough" win
6. Hale-___ comet
7. One-touch phone feature
8. 1999-2004 Olds model
9. Having a sophisticated charm
10. Emergency procedure, briefly
11. Kitchen necessity
13. Cheese similar to Parmesan
19. "My country ___ of thee"
21. Big name in soups
23. Abbr. after "Cleveland" or "Shaker"
24. "Tie a Yellow Ribbon" tree
25. High seriousness
27. Fever reading
29. "Big Blue" computer company
30. Bandleader Brown of renown

33. Aachen assent
35. Acclaimed Dadaist
38. Chalet overhangs
40. Equal to face value
41. Financial news network
42. Bar Mitzvah dance

43. Exactly as required
45. Kickstarter number
46. Charitable handouts
47. Fall mo.
50. Breakfast for Brutus, perhaps

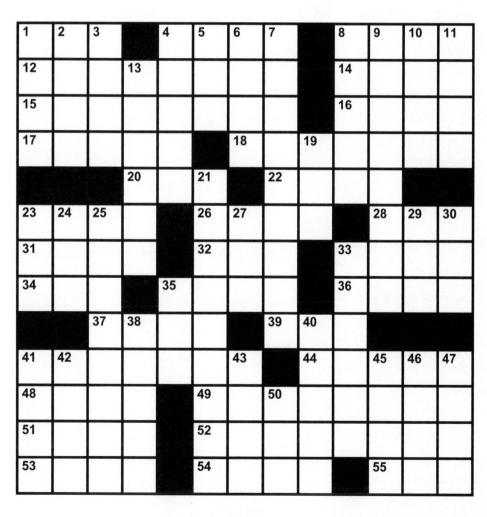

Answers on page 176.

FICTIONAL PLACES

ACROSS

1. Computer port
4. "Sonic the Hedgehog" developer
8. Apartment in London
12. "America the Beautiful" closer
13. Aspirin, e.g.
14. Candy in a cylindrical package
15. Dry red wine
17. "Beetle Bailey" dog
18. Exotic jelly fruit
19. Like a clay pot
21. Home of Queen Eliz.
23. Boardroom graphic
24. "Lost Horizon" paradise
29. Rock's ___ Speedwagon
30. Drawn tight
31. Caviar, literally
32. Treasure site in "It's a Mad, Mad, Mad, Mad World"
33. 9-1-1 responder
34. Musical's mystical village
36. Far from poetic
38. Big Columbus sch.
39. Egyptian monarch who abdicated in 1952
42. Eniwetok first
46. Anita of jazz fame
47. Wolf in sheep's clothing, e.g.
49. Costa follower
50. Glide like a buzzard
51. It may be positively charged
52. Bambi's aunts
53. Actress Ione
54. ___-Caps (Nestle candy)

DOWN

1. Govt. shore patrol
2. 12-time Pro Bowl player Junior
3. Ali of "Arabian Nights"
4. Leapt suddenly
5. "Ich Bin ___ Berliner": JFK
6. Fox program about a choir
7. Rival of Aspen
8. Foamy cover
9. Fictional ladies' man
10. Bruce Banner, to the Hulk
11. Fictional city in "Who Framed Roger Rabbit?" (1988)
16. Gala or ball
20. "His Master's Voice" record label
22. Angry dog's warning
24. Fictional town with robotic wives
25. Amateur broadcaster's gear
26. Event for Foyt
27. Dalmatian number
28. Big brand of blocks

32. Buffalo Wild Wings nickname based on its initials

34. Mitt Romney's alma mater, for short

35. How some shells are washed

37. Tofu beans

40. Barely touch, on a pool table

41. "Fine here"

43. "(Sittin' on) the Dock of the Bay" singer Redding

44. 12 men have walked on it

45. Capital of Moravia

48. Wages

1	2	3		4	5	6	7		8	9	10	11
12				13					14			
15			16						17			
18						19		20				
			21		22			23				
24	25	26				27	28			29		
30					31				32			
33				34				35				
36			37				38					
39					40	41		42		43	44	45
46					47		48					
49					50					51		
52					53					54		

Answers on page 176.

RHYME TIME

ACROSS

1. Office furniture
5. Wood used for skis
8. List on a product label
12. Home of some Bruins
13. Elton's john?
14. Hatcher of Hollywood
15. "How now, ___?"
17. Leave out
18. Girlie makeup?
20. Fleming who created Oddjob
21. Lamb pen name
22. Friendly TV alien
25. Saverin who co-founded Facebook
28. Opposites on Santa's list
32. Intimidate
33. Home movie purchase
34. Stitch's pal
35. Mumbai "mister"
38. Chancy undertaking
44. Profoundly wicked
45. It's a long story
46. Woody scent
47. Sundown, in sonnets
48. Keyed up
49. Frankfort's river
50. Football scores
51. Thor, Zeus, etc.

DOWN

1. Taps with a sword
2. Sandy brown color
3. Walk with effort
4. Japanese piano maker
5. Old road to Fairbanks
6. Anytime now
7. Folksy greeting
8. Like a perfect world
9. Dryish
10. Clapton or Idle
11. Surfer's stop
16. Gun-lobby grp.
19. Insulting comment
22. Year in San Juan
23. Shrunken head?
24. Tank-to-engine conduit
25. Sight seer
26. 605, to Caesar
27. Venerable reference bk.
29. One presiding at the barbecue
30. Angelic symbol
31. Biped's claim to fame
35. Brats' targets
36. Kind of room, for short
37. Convention clip-on
38. "___ Man," '83 Estevez film
39. "The Art of Love" poet

40. Festooned mischievously

41. "Othello" villain

42. Lummox

43. Brain tests, briefly

1	2	3	4		5	6	7		8	9	10	11
12					13				14			
15			16						17			
18							19					
		20				21						
22	23	24			25				26	27		
28		29	30	31								
32								33				
	34					35	36	37				
38	39				40				41	42	43	
44				45								
46			47				48					
49			50				51					

Answers on page 177.

DRIVING AROUND

ACROSS

1. Back-talking
8. Went for a rebound, say
13. "Same here"
14. Hyper
15. Most dubious
16. Plant equivalent of blood vessels
17. Shoe-size letters
18. "Forbidden" perfume
20. Passing try, in football stats
21. Amusement park vehicle
24. Three-R's org.
25. Lee Greenwood's "God Bless the ___"
26. Nervous or solar ___
28. Bat an eyelash, say
31. Greenish-blue shades
32. Like royal descent, usually
34. Camera shot
35. Ex of Mickey, Artie, and Frank
36. Musical symbol
41. Annual Asian holiday
42. Change one's story?
43. To be, with you
44. ___ acid (mild antiseptic)
46. Missing something
49. "___ Gay" (famous B-29)
50. Anti
51. Stave off

52. Prairie homes

DOWN

1. It's rarely a hit
2. Farewell, to Francoise
3. Command to Fido
4. Star Wars initials
5. Suffix with social or suburban
6. Cosa ___
7. Scored a "gentleman's grade"
8. Lincoln or Infiniti, e.g.
9. Tarzan player Ron
10. Peach Bowl site
11. Like a 12-year-old
12. Large orchestral gongs
19. Humanities degs.
22. Faultless
23. What the British call a station wagon
27. In ___ (on the same page)
28. Tow truck type
29. Easy mark
30. Racing, as pacers
33. Set the pace
34. Thick, creamy soup
37. Bite lightly, as a puppy might
38. "I Believe" singer Frankie
39. Wipe away, as chalk
40. Some hat materials

45. Land in the Seine

47. Music's Carly ___ Jepsen

48. Gratuity

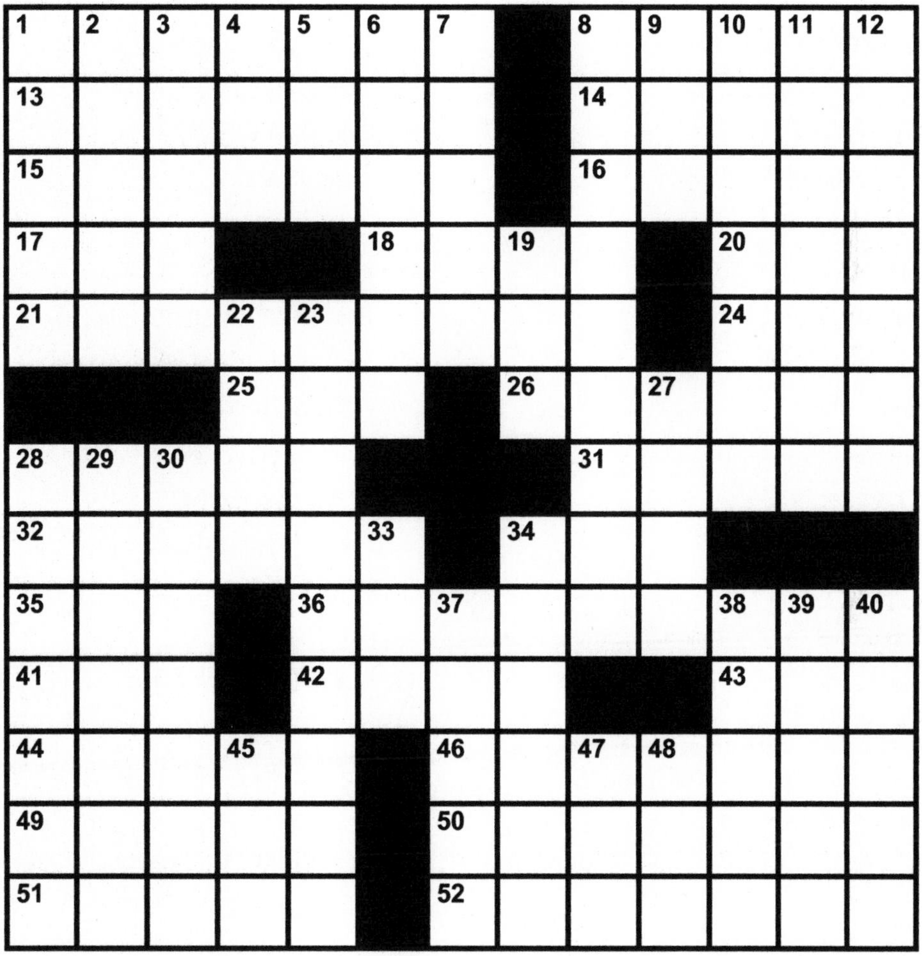

Answers on page 177.

ADVERTISING MASCOTS

ACROSS

1. Angler's buy
4. Quite a ways away
7. Goblet, for example
12. Sushi-bar soybean
14. Hall's musical partner
15. No longer working
16. An inedible orange
17. Former mascot for corn chips
19. New Jersey city at the eastern end of I-80
20. Small unit of force
23. Overhead light
24. Treehouse builder, often
27. Kennedy or Kerry of Massachusetts
29. Letter ender
31. "Live from New York!" initials
32. Old superpower
36. Christmas concert tune
37. Natural sugar
39. Spaghetti-in-a-can icon
44. Resident of a gulf state
45. Foolishness
46. Pop singer Lavigne
47. Split end
48. Che's chum
49. Fed. ID
50. Journal or Japan finish

DOWN

1. Maker of foam toys
2. Linda of Broadway's "Jekyll & Hyde"
3. Comedic filmmaker Jacques
4. Denmark's ___ Islands
5. One-celled organisms
6. Tiny biter
7. Pent-up emotion reliever
8. Eye surgery acronym
9. Rat- follower (gun sound)
10. Utah's state flower
11. Boston-to-Nantucket dir.
13. Hand holder?
18. USA's largest labor union
20. Platter spinners, for short
21. Hither's companion
22. Oiler's org.
24. Thelma and Louise, e.g.
25. Sendak's "Where the Wild Things ___"
26. High-speed connection, briefly
28. Carry out
30. Like a close ball game
33. Aquatic vessel
34. Shows derision
35. Queens and princes
37. Aladdin associate
38. Chief evil
39. 906, in Roman numerals

40. Like diamonds

41. Netherlands sight

42. Summers in Europe

43. Jane in a Bronte title

44. Graceless sort

Answers on page 177.

13-LETTER WORDS

ACROSS

1. Dog, cat or hamster
4. Baby sheep
8. Certain hotel amenity
12. "4," sometimes: abbr.
13. Actor Morales
14. " ___ and the King of Siam"
15. "Blame It On ___" (Caine movie)
16. 75 percent, say
17. "Diga Diga Doo" trio
18. Professional needler?
21. It sounds like "air"
22. Fair way to divide things
23. Ages, as tobacco
26. Bikini half
27. All-even score
28. "Author unknown": Abbr.
29. "Anthem" author Rand
30. Prefix meaning "ten"
31. Bull Run soldier
32. Aspiring Ph.D.'s test
33. Less dotty
34. For the time being, in Latin
36. Former "Buffy the Vampire Slayer" network
37. Bird-watcher
42. Currency unit in Iran
43. Sign of a skunk
44. Big name in video games
45. Anchored fastener
46. Place where salt is found
47. "___ be my pleasure!"
48. Bilko and Snorkel
49. Startled squeals
50. "Born as"

DOWN

1. Legal assistant, for short
2. "Aeneid" or "Iliad"
3. Bad thing to drop in public
4. Wide-eyed primates of Madagascar
5. In concert
6. Opposite of fem.
7. Heron relative
8. "M*A*S*H" chaplain
9. Certain long odds
10. Common pizzeria order
11. Just over 12 months ago
19. Back end of a hammer
20. Cavaliers' sch.
23. Sedan shelters
24. Consistently accurate
25. Johnson Space Center humanoid project
26. Terse ta-ta
29. Sleeve feature

30. "Rats!"

32. See the point of

33. Combination utensils

35. Pinball no-nos

36. Horseshoe-shaped bike protector

38. "Garfield" beagle

39. "Bingo!"

40. .com location

41. Wave maker

1	2	3	■	4	5	6	7	■	8	9	10	11
12			■	13				■	14			
15			■	16				■	17			
18			19				20					
■	■	■	21			■	22					
23	24	25			■	26			■	27		
28			■	29			■	30				
31			■	32			■	33				
34			35			■	36			■	■	■
37					38				39	40	41	
42				■	43				■	44		
45				■	46				■	47		
48				■	49				■	50		

Answers on page 177.

__ HO!

ACROSS

1. "Field of Dreams" setting
5. Getting on
8. Whip
12. Sporty car roof
13. Seven, on a sundial
14. Diva's solo
15. Farmer's acreage
17. Break a habit
18. Buddy of rock fame
19. Harry Potter's country
21. "___ and whose army?"
23. Baby's "piggy"
24. "Que Sera, Sera" singer Doris
27. Apprehend, as a perp
29. Basket twig
33. A round cheese
35. Free (of)
37. A few or more
38. Dried coconut meat
40. Auction gesture
42. Bar bowl item
43. Audiophile's collection
45. Acrobat catcher
47. Floral crown
51. Norman Bates is a good example of one
55. A lake or canal
56. New Zealand's most populous city
58. "At Last" singer James
59. Navy noncom
60. "Good heavens!"
61. "Peachy ___!"
62. Barrel at a bash
63. Boomers' kids, briefly

DOWN

1. Calamine lotion target
2. Another, in Madrid
3. Blanket material
4. Put on, as makeup
5. Caesar's eggs
6. "I Walk the ___," Cash hit
7. Failed to do
8. Like the Wild West of yore
9. Conspiracy buff's ___ 51
10. Actress Phillips of "I, Claudius"
11. Clock part
16. Home to French silk makers
20. Baby talk word
22. '50s Mideast alliance
24. Big mo. for toy stores
25. "Much ___ About Nothing"
26. Bark annoyingly
28. Bargain holder, maybe
30. Atom with a charge
31. Aussie coat-of-arms bird

32. Like professors emeritus: abbr.

34. Magic Eraser spokesman

36. "American Pie" McLean

39. "Give Kids A Smile" org.

41. Newspaper's city ___

44. Cheese and crackers, e.g.

46. Bathroom-cleaner brand

47. Adorkable one

48. Commedia dell'___ (improvised comedy)

49. Baptism or confirmation, e.g.

50. Copy, for short

52. Actor Nicolas

53. Burl in wood

54. "Against All ___" (Phil Collins #1 hit)

57. Gear piece

1	2	3	4		5	6	7		8	9	10	11
12					13				14			
15				16					17			
18						19		20				
			21		22		23					
24	25	26		27		28		29		30	31	32
33			34		35		36		37			
38				39		40		41		42		
			43		44		45		46			
47	48	49				50		51		52	53	54
55					56		57					
58					59				60			
61					62				63			

Answers on page 178.

FAMILY ENTERTAINMENT

ACROSS

1. The Queen of Country Music
9. What a rejected lover carries
10. Flies off the handle
11. Going by plane
13. Coffee holder
14. Daughter-in-law of 1-Across
18. "Keystone" figure
19. Targets of football kicks
21. Gun barrel blade
23. Come out ahead of
24. Song recorded by 1-Across and 14-Across in 2007

DOWN

2. Baseball boo-boo
3. Butt collector
4. Animation unit
5. Like a twangy voice
6. Crickets and beetles
7. Consume completely
8. Tear into
12. Country estate
15. Fake it, musically
16. Steals from
17. Absentee ticket holder
18. Barbecue favorite
19. Big name in knives
20. Altercation
22. Ascot, for example

Answers on page 178.

PULL

ACROSS

1. She played a medical engineer in 13-Across
8. Records another performer's song
9. Babe in arms
10. Description of a very small town
12. Where fabric pieces meet
13. 2013 sci-fi movie title that means "pull"
17. Oxide or ointment type
18. Aggressive market competition
19. Charity sale
20. "No need to explain"
22. He played the team commander in 13-Across

DOWN

2. Bottom line
3. She's a deer
4. "Sound of Music" setting
5. Act as one
6. The way you pass your days
7. Scam artist
11. Tot's mealtime perch
14. First letter
15. Jolly Roger flier
16. Mad magazine piece, e.g.
18. Pocketbook
21. Logical beginning

Answers on page 178.

THE BREAKFAST CLUB

ACROSS

1. He played "the athlete" Andy in "The Breakfast Club"
8. Gridlock cause
9. Place to wash up
10. Brazilian vacation spot
11. Optional courses
13. Ally, who played "the basket case" Allison in "The Breakfast Club"
15. Judd, who played "the criminal" John in "The Breakfast Club"
18. Source of sweets
19. "Dig in!"
20. Like luxury car interiors
22. Gliding ballroom dance
23. She played "the princess" Claire in "The Breakfast Club"

DOWN

1. Gets by coercion
2. Baking potato
3. Short stop or second baseman
4. Go over
5. Key for indenting
6. In relation to
7. Cheap shots, e.g.
12. "Those Were the Days," to "All in the Family"
14. Chinese appetizer
16. Journalist's tablet
17. Drink with an umbrella, often
18. Play a ukelele
19. Actor in a crowd
21. "That's great news!"

Answers on page 178.

IT'S ALL IN HOW YOU READ IT

ACROSS

1. "The King of Queens" actress Remini
5. "___ good turn daily" (Boy Scouts slogan)
8. Lots
12. "Alice's Restaurant" singer Guthrie
13. Caterer's coffee server
14. David and Goliath's battlefield
15. Former SNL star Kristen
16. "Give ___ break!"
17. Aloha State bird
18. Where you live—or bully next door?
21. Author Chinua Achebe, by birth
22. "Homeland" agcy.
23. Bit of statuary
26. DVD forerunner
27. Bacon feature
30. "Could be trouble!"
31. How-to letters
32. "Fiddlesticks!"
33. "Didn't need to hear that!"
34. Sugar snap
35. Came up
36. Archer's asset
37. The Gay Nineties, e.g.
38. Below the level of awareness—or thinking about a long sandwich?
44. Burkina ___ (African nation)

45. "Teletubbies" fan
46. Prefix meaning "skin"
47. Allowed to mellow
48. Burgundy summer
49. Ecto's opposite
50. Air Force outpost
51. "Gidget" star Sandra
52. Ex-QB Flutie

DOWN

1. Croquet play area
2. Huron neighbor
3. Et ___ ("and others")
4. Greedy—or keep actress Lillian all to yourself?
5. Beloved Disney elephant
6. "Got Milk?" ad partner
7. Complete lawlessness
8. Birthplace of Columbus
9. Alternative spread
10. Merry Men unit
11. Junk, to a sailor
19. "Game of Thrones" cable channel
20. Grafton's "___ for Homicide"
23. "Boy king" of Egypt
24. Bit of resistance
25. Bourbon ruler
26. By way of

27. Egg ___ Yung
28. "A Midsummer Night's Dream" disguise
29. "That'll be ___ day!"
31. Kicked downstairs
32. Like pigtails—or recognized bikini top?
34. Apt rhyme for "flick"
35. Boomerang's path
36. "Humble" dwelling

37. Beauty expert Lauder
38. "Beowulf," for one
39. Doesn't allow to gather dust
40. Brief reminder
41. Prefix meaning "wine"
42. Hindu language
43. Air pollutant
44. "The ___ Four" (The Beatles)

1	2	3	4		5	6	7		8	9	10	11
12					13				14			
15					16				17			
18			19				20					
		21				22						
23	24	25			26				27	28	29	
30				31				32				
33				34				35				
		36				37						
	38	39			40				41	42	43	
44					45				46			
47					48				49			
50					51				52			

61

Answers on page 179.

GONE FISHIN'

ACROSS

1. Catch for a grizzly
7. Largest mammals
13. "Have a sample!"
14. Repetitive way to learn
15. Desdemona's love, in opera
16. Litter holder
17. London theater district
19. 6-point football scores
20. Auto supplier for the Swedish royal family
21. Aquarium favorite
24. Conger's catch
27. Sheriff-badge shape
29. Big bosses
30. Brilliantly colored flower
32. Oak tree wannabes
34. Backyard tree dangler
35. Abrasive soap brand
37. Posed for pix
38. In the cereal bowl too long, maybe
40. Business letter addressees
42. "Mer" makeup
43. Processor created by Apple, IBM and Motorola
47. Cuba's Fidel or Raul
50. ___ Beach (California resort)
51. First stages
52. Joe Lieberman's middle name
53. Recess rebuttal, perhaps
54. Cocktail crustacean

DOWN

1. Do pier work
2. Comedian Johnson of "Laugh-In"
3. Caustics in soaps
4. Casts off the skin
5. Like some condos
6. Hospital unit for newborns
7. Pugilism org.
8. Hilton rival
9. Chrysler Building's style
10. Maine delicacies
11. Area commanded by DDE
12. Gender
18. Alias, for a co.
22. "Mazes and Monsters" writer Jaffe
23. 2nd in charge
24. Beanery sign
25. Basso Pinza of "South Pacific"
26. Generosity
28. Stuffed Italian pockets
31. Papal envoys
33. Something to roll up your windows for
36. "Little Orphan Annie" bodyguard with "the"

39. Mongolian tents

41. "Popeye" creator

44. Fashion designer Gernreich

45. ___ Penh, Cambodia's capital (variant)

46. Complain about a fish dinner?

47. Boston trademark

48. Munich : Jahr :: Madrid : ___

49. Baja bear

Answers on page 179.

GETTING ARTY

ACROSS

1. Big shot in hockey
5. "West Point of the South"
8. Cocktail napkin jotting
12. Act like a couch potato
13. "In one ___ and out the other"
14. "Happy Gilmore" actor Sandler
15. Certain tennis edge
16. Defrosts
18. It features religious symbolism
20. Barbara Bush, ___ Pierce
21. "___ Never Fall in Love Again"
22. BP merger partner
25. Chum
26. Jr. Olympic Games sponsor
29. The oldest known go back 44,000 years
32. 2.95, for Don Drysdale
33. Any top 10 song, say
34. Cause of kitchen tears
35. Comical Olive
36. "How peculiar"
37. It includes street art and any art of today
43. City across the Peace Bridge from Buffalo
44. Body part that may be hazel
45. "Cabaret" star Minnelli
46. Canoe paddle
47. Carpenter's clamp
48. At the crest of
49. "No Such Agency" agcy.
50. "Jekyll & Hyde" actress Linda or German river.

DOWN

1. Bacon hunk
2. Gaga or Godiva
3. Comedian Ansari
4. Way of showing repentance
5. Classic Chevy, briefly
6. Hawaiian fish, for short
7. From Tehran, say
8. Congested-sounding
9. Floral emanation
10. Far from slack
11. Paramedic, for short
17. Comfortably off
19. Greenhorn
22. I or II, in blackjack
23. Spoil, as a finish
24. Fertility lab supply
25. Area for an orchestra
26. "As Is" singer DiFranco
27. Ages ___ (time long past)
28. Adm.'s outfit
30. Airplane's wing flap

31. Ready to roll, as a car
35. Available for immediate use
36. "Aida" or "Carmen," e.g.
37. San Francisco's ___ Tower
38. Itsy-bitsy pasta

39. Actresses Farrow and Sara
40. Desert descriptor
41. "All ___!" (court command)
42. River of Flanders
43. Cape Canaveral's st.

1	2	3	4	■	5	6	7	■	8	9	10	11
12				■	13			■	14			
15				■	16		17					
18			19								■	■
■	■	20			■	21			■			■
22	23	24			■	25			■	26	27	28
29				30			31					
32		■	33			■	34					
■	■	35			■	36			■	■		
	37	38			39				40	41	42	
43						■	44					
45			■	46			47					
48			■	49			50					

Answers on page 179.

FINISH THE ADAGE (2)

ACROSS

1. Multiple Grammy winner Mitchell
5. A wool producer
8. Medical Mehmet
12. "The dismal science," briefly
13. Mark, as a ballot square
14. Pitchwoman ___ Lenska
15. Ready money
17. Sacred bird of the Nile
18. Don't call . . . (finish the adage)
20. Beloved animal
21. It means nothing
22. Sports bar fixture, for short
25. Hovercraft, for short
26. "Do the ___" (beverage slogan)
29. Forbidden fruit...(finish the adage)
32. "Deck the Halls" contraction
33. Be sorry about
34. Puts the kibosh on
35. Apiece
36. Amt. of sugar
37. Look . . . (finish the adage)
44. A toast topper
45. Meet by chance
46. Brake component, often
47. Golfing great Ernie
48. Showdown time
49. Funnyman Rogen
50. "___War": Shatner novel
51. "Love and Squalor" girl

DOWN

1. King of Israel known for his furious chariot attacks
2. Andes tubers
3. Oslo's loc.
4. Like serious reporting
5. Give high praise
6. Cheesehead's st.
7. Change for the better
8. Dental tool
9. Color of some hummingbird throats
10. A miscellany
11. Old-time actress Pitts
16. More shrewd
19. Animates
22. English ___ (college course)
23. CBS hit drama set in Vegas
24. Some NFL linemen
25. "Wow" kind of feeling
26. Jazz saxophonist Gordon, familiarly
27. Away from WNW
28. Barbells, etc.
30. It can't fail
31. A call here may lead to an arrest
35. Four-legged friend

36. Siberian city established under Boris Godunov
37. Muscle Beach displays
38. Nobel Laureate Wiesel
39. Word with gab or October

40. Christmas log
41. "Dukes of Hazzard" deputy
42. Basic biological building block
43. Bread in Southern cuisine

1	2	3	4		5	6	7		8	9	10	11
12					13				14			
15				16					17			
18								19				
			20				21					
22	23	24				25				26	27	28
29					30				31			
32				33				34				
			35				36					
37	38	39				40				41	42	43
44					45							
46					47				48			
49					50				51			

Answers on page 179.

THE NEXT BIG THING

ACROSS

1. Big, big, big
8. "___ la vista!"
13. Put in danger
14. "The Enemy Below" threat
15. Abraham's Oscar-winning role
16. Former Golden Arches burger
17. Greek letters
18. Big fuss
20. "Carte" or "mode" preceder
21. Big name in home dyes
22. "___ Tag" (German greeting)
23. 52, to Caesar
24. "___ Hard" (Willis film)
25. Most common family name in Vietnam
27. Colorado snowboarding mecca
30. Newspaper opinion pieces
31. He found the Pacific
33. French noble
34. A dozen eggs, in a lab
35. Branch, to a botanist
37. 180 degrees from NNW
40. Computer network acronym
41. "Just the facts, ___"
42. Low-lying wetland
43. Beginner's course
45. Juice brand owned by Coca-Cola

47. Impolite army acronym meaning "a big mess"
48. Like bankruptcy, maybe
49. Listens attentively
50. Mammoth

DOWN

1. Penny-pincher
2. Classic violin maker
3. Bug-on-the-windshield noise
4. Mexico City half-dozen
5. Angry emotion
6. Faith, hope, or charity
7. "Do I dare to eat a peach?" poet
8. Gigantic
9. "Jeopardy!" airer
10. Soap-making solution
11. Kept score
12. Gains through effort
19. Lion's hangout
22. Hyperbolically large
24. Ball gal
26. Bar code: Abbr.
27. Make illegal
28. Rhino's realm
29. Relating to the sole
32. 1.5-volt battery size
33. Soft-nosed bullet

36. Native New Zealander
37. Athenian law-giver
38. Stage direction that means "alone"
39. Backspace over text

42. A pride of lions?
44. Jack's Attorney General, initially
46. "Paris, Texas" director Wenders

1	2	3	4	5	6	7		8	9	10	11	12
13								14				
15								16				
17					18		19			20		
21				22					23			
			24				25		26			
27	28	29						30				
31					32		33					
34				35		36				37	38	39
40				41					42			
43			44			45		46				
47						48						
49						50						

Answers on page 180.

12-STRING GUITAR

ACROSS

1. 1965 Rolling Stones song with a 12-string guitar
7. Line made with a compass
8. Everybody
9. "Be my guest"
11. Respond to a sneeze
12. Beatles song with a 12-string guitar
16. Barely warm
18. California redwood
20. For each person
22. Skillet for stir fry
23. 1969 David Bowie song with a 12-string guitar

DOWN

1. Beyond passe
2. Hidden treasure
3. Improve wine or cheese
4. Barrier that bumps boat bottoms
5. Speak pompously
6. Cheerleader output
7. Feeling of dread
10. Fusses over, with "on"
13. Chess climax
14. ID checker's post
15. Flat-fixing tool
16. Bloopers in books
17. Arctic jacket
19. "Sort of" prefix
21. Not a Rep. nor a Dem.

Answers on page 180.

FIND THE CITY

ACROSS

1. Environmental condition in a Peruvian city?
8. Hose in a shell, once
13. Footsteps sound
14. Under-the-sink pipe
15. 1991 Steve Martin film set in Calif.
16. In need of an update
17. ICU part
18. Subject to change
20. To put something somewhere
22. "I get it now" sounds
23. Agent of Uncle Sam
24. Big name in health plans
26. Hugs, in a letter
27. Amuse greatly
30. Driving reversals
33. "Fifth Beatle" Yoko
34. Diplomatic negotiations
36. Mo. for an apple festival
37. Cookie holder
38. "I wish I were an ___ Mayer wiener"
42. Swinging around
44. Alley Oop's abode
45. "The Language of Clothes" author Alison
46. Classic mouthwash
49. Taking too much, for short
50. Fence in
51. Dandelions, e.g.
52. Lack the courage to include a Nevada city?

DOWN

1. A little better than average
2. "Weekend Edition Sunday" host ___ Hansen
3. "Let ___ where it is"
4. Tool similar to a pickax
5. GI address letters
6. Black sticky stuff
7. Original form of a word
8. Strong cravings
9. "Call My Name" jazz singer James
10. Try to seize, as the gold ring
11. Mexican city found in an old warship?
12. Racer's swimwear
19. Big name in rental trucks
21. Zero, in soccer scores
25. "Hop on!"
27. Norwegian city seen not keeping up?
28. Count in
29. Pennsylvania city found in a circle of friends?
31. Bout ender, for short
32. Destroyer attacked in Aden in Oct., 2000

35. Fished with a hook

37. 1970s supermodel Cheryl

39. "Gigi" star Leslie

40. French message-carrying boat

41. Adjust one's watch

43. Air force?

47. Actress and comic Gasteyer

48. '70s tape player

1	2	3	4	5	6	7		8	9	10	11	12
13								14				
15								16				
17						18	19					
20				21		22				23		
			24		25					26		
27	28	29					30	31	32			
33					34	35						
36				37				38		39	40	41
42			43						44			
45						46	47	48				
49						50						
51						52						

Answers on page 180.

SIR RICHARD

ACROSS

1. 1993 film including Sir Richard
8. Bucket go-with
9. Hidden feature in a computer game or DVD
10. "Gandhi" setting
11. "Take care of that!"
12. 1977 film directed by Sir Richard
16. Unwelcome information
18. Gold star
20. Lose one's cool
22. Feeling poorly
23. Actor/director Sir Richard

DOWN

1. Montego Bay's island
2. Extremely quick
3. Airline employee
4. Brainpower ratings
5. Jigsaw element
6. Recite effortlessly
7. "And this is the thanks ___?"
11. Boils slowly
13. Minuteman's enemy
14. Rampaging
15. Santa's lead reindeer
16. Bassinet occupant
17. Backspace over
19. "Goodbye, cheri!"
21. City area, for short

Answers on page 180.

A PAIR OF MOVIES

ACROSS

1. 2014 sci-fi film set in a postapocalyptic future
6. Boar's mate
8. Inn offering a meal, for short
9. Camper's water flask
10. Go separate ways
11. Bring up the rear
12. Devastating blow
14. Brunch egg dish
17. Again and again
19. Convenient kind of shopping
22. Furthest ebb
23. Cease-fire
24. "The King and I" star Brynner
25. 2015 sequel to 1-Acoss

DOWN

1. Charger's woes
2. "Plain" flavor
3. Bomb squad machine
4. Avoid capture
5. "A Christmas Carol" boy
6. "I'm outta here!"
7. Kate of this puzzle's two movies
12. Shailene of this puzzle's two movies
13. "Moon River" composer
15. BLT ingredient
16. Celestial streakers
18. Absorbent cloth
20. Walk in
21. Fabric fold

Answers on page 181.

EVEN AS WE SPOCK

ACROSS

1. Series hosted by Leonard Nimoy
6. Was humbled
7. Up and about
9. Underworld river
10. Sci-fi series in which Nimoy played Spock
12. Beach near Omaha
13. Postseason gridiron game
18. Start of a catch phrase of Spock
20. Blue green shade
22. Get-acquainted event
23. Statement of surrender
24. End of the catch phrase

DOWN

1. Playful words to a toddler
2. Comedy routine
3. Highly perceptive
4. Cyberspace place
5. How the elated walk
6. As well
8. Lodge members
11. Postal receptacle
14. After-dinner drink
15. Chowder choice
16. Deep blue
17. Access for a wheelchair
19. One of Santa's reindeer
21. Barely noticeable amount

Answers on page 181.

HIDDEN CLUE

ACROSS

1. Fleeting success
8. Asian archipelago
9. Bench press target
10. Light haircut
11. Large amphibian
14. Characteristic of a Type A
16. Excuse designed to elicit tears
18. Spoiled kid
21. Neither's companion
22. Middleman
24. Saver of nine

DOWN

1. Act the coquette
2. Confusing
3. Word for "clue" hidden in the three long answers
4. Denials
5. Without deliberation
6. Hamelin's rat catcher, for one
7. Last place finisher, proverbially
12. Absolute
13. "Don't go anywhere!"
14. Shout of praise
15. Haifa inhabitant
17. Military cap
19. Subtle coloration
20. Nonlethal phaser setting
23. Expression of disdain

Answers on page 181.

GOOD-BYE, GOOD BUY

ACROSS

1. Good buy
9. Bargain-priced
10. Publicly criticize
11. Evaluated
12. A burning desire?
13. Good-bye
15. Ancient empire of Asia
18. Room at the top
20. Good buy
23. Bing Crosby, for one
24. Olympics award
25. Good-bye

DOWN

2. Twisted treat
3. Matchmaker with wings
4. Endure without protest
5. Off with permission
6. Adult polliwogs
7. Building with a dome
8. "Bullets" in poker
13. Ouija board meetings
14. "Sorry, that's not possible!"
16. Stunt double, for one
17. Spain plus Portugal
19. Hidden treasure
21. Shakespearean loverboy
22. Cairo river

Answers on page 181.

THE AMERICANS

ACROSS

1. Philip portrayer in Joe Weisberg's "The Americans"
8. Blush
9. Latin dance
10. "To A Skylark," e.g.
11. "Do whatever you want"
13. Espionage novel by Joe Weisberg, who created "The Americans"
16. Prove to be competent
19. "Sure thing"
21. One way to cook clams
22. Be unfaithful to
23. Elizabeth portrayer in Joe Weisberg's "The Americans"

DOWN

1. D.C. subway
2. Hit man
3. "Ready or not, ___ come"
4. Roll of bills
5. Exercise wheel runner
6. "Lion King" cub
7. Foxworthy's field
12. Pound part
13. "Close, but no cigar!"
14. Ringo, for one
15. Do a free fall
17. Smart ___
18. Blizzard equipment
20. Bloodhound's clue
22. Adhesive for feathers

Answers on page 182.

MISNOMERS

ACROSS

1. Holy pilgrimage
5. Fireside chat pres.
8. Diva's big moment
12. A lightbulb can represent it
13. "Blame It on ___" (Michael Caine flick)
14. Club or baking follower
15. They aren't for parking and don't lead to parks
17. Junior in the NFL Hall of Fame
18. Confess, with "up"
19. Last word of "America the Beautiful"
21. They were invented by mathematicians in India
28. Bored, with "up"
29. 3, on sundials
30. Earth miniature
31. Aladdin's find
33. "Game, ___, match!"
35. Brit's subway
36. "Pong" company
38. Massage
40. "A mouse!"
41. They were so named for dogs, not birds
44. A pitcher wants a low one, for short
45. Pigeon call
46. Mine entrance
49. It's actually bright orange

54. Chore list topper
55. "___ voyage!"
56. Main river of Switzerland
57. Celestial hammerer
58. No specific one
59. A bit less than a meter

DOWN

1. "___ to Be Square" (Huey Lewis and the News hit)
2. Cavity-fighting org.
3. German "the"
4. Bob Dylan's youngest son
5. Drake the navigator
6. Abbr. for a handy-andy
7. "Martini and ___"
8. Battery partner
9. Fishy eggs
10. "Sweet" girl of songdom
11. Org. that sponsors the Junior Olympics
16. 1939-45 event, briefly
20. "Deviled" food
21. Company with a "spokesduck"
22. Calf catcher
23. Commercial creator
24. Celebrity chef Guy ___
25. Capital of Normandy
26. Died down

27. Is on the lookout for
32. Roman magistrate
34. Region whose capital is Florence
37. Discount clothing tag abbr.
39. Allied nations
42. Start of a "Flintstones" shout
43. Good to go
46. Big inits. in long distance
47. "Dumb, dumb, dumb!" to Homer Simpson
48. Affirmative at the altar
50. Actor Chaney, Jr.
51. Barnyard bleat
52. Bobby of hockey fame
53. Crossed (out)

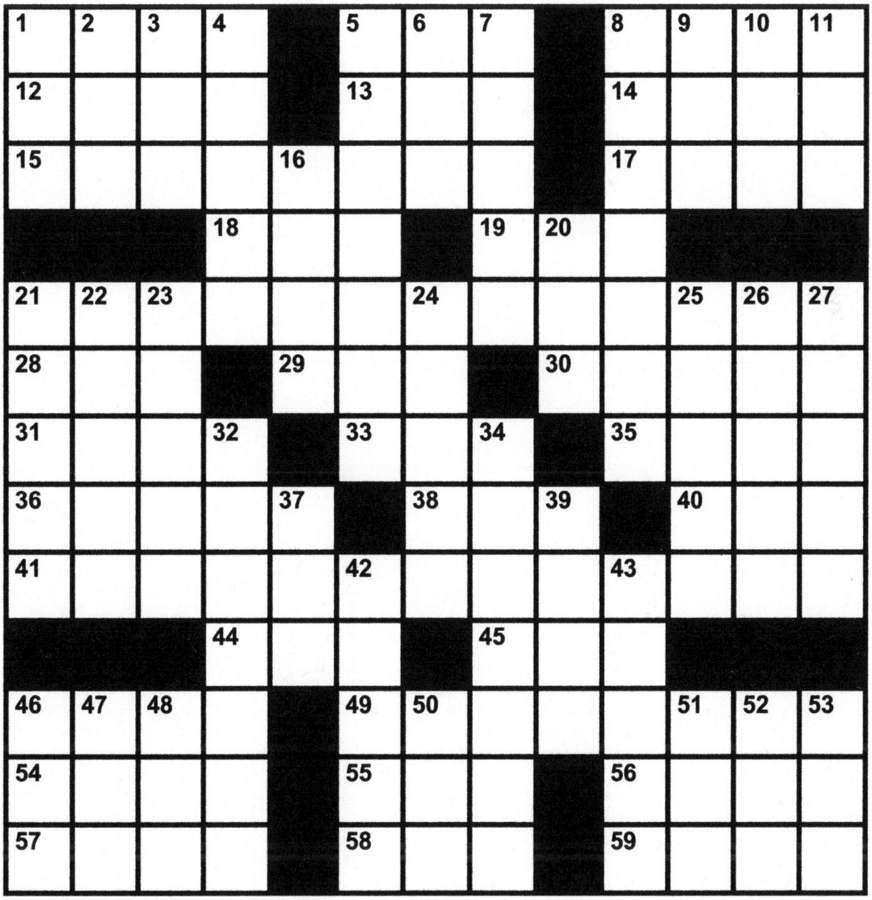
1
2
3
4
5
6
7
8
9
10
11
12
13
14
15
16
17
18
19
20
21
22
23
24
25
26
27
28
29
30
31
32
33
34
35
36
37
38
39
40
41
42
43
44
45
46
47
48
49
50
51
52
53
54
55
56
57
58
59

Answers on page 182.

ROCK AND ROLL HALL OF FAME

ACROSS

1. "Blue Monday" singer in the Rock and Roll Hall of Fame
8. With ice cream
9. "Northern Exposure" animal
10. I problem
11. Done in desperation
13. "Tutti Frutti" singer in the Rock and Roll Hall of Fame
16. Plain, refreshing drink
19. '50s White House nickname
21. Arouse, as feelings
22. Close-fitting sleeveless shirt
23. "Johnny B. Goode" singer in the Rock and Roll Hall of Fame

DOWN

1. Pilot light
2. Unfreeze
3. Whimsically humorous
4. Sultry West
5. Prone to wandering
6. "Whatever floats your ___"
7. School of acting
12. Walk with swagger
13. Case on a necklace
14. Engineered simply
15. Cockpit occupant
17. Circus cat
18. Some Motown music, for short
20. Like a nest syndrome
22. Breath mint word

Answers on page 182.

TWO MEN AND A LOVELY LADY

ACROSS

1. 1990 movie with Julia Roberts
8. Home to a queen
9. Slightest residue
10. Style of jazz
11. Casual conversation
13. Director of 1-Across
17. Story used to sell suds
19. Gentle touch
20. Two trios and a duo
21. Evict forcefully, say
22. Leading man in 1-Across

DOWN

1. Marshy place
2. "Dig in!"
3. In need of a drink
4. "Star Trek: TNG" alum Wheaton
5. "Heavy" music
6. Horseshoe Falls location
7. Quick pull
12. Astonish, as grace
14. Atomic energy unit
15. Clams and oysters
16. 1970 Beatles chart-topper
17. Come in third
18. Eye related
19. Bell's invention
21. Feathery neckwear

Answers on page 182.

HODGEPODGE

ACROSS

1. Lucifer, for one
7. Irritating insect
8. "Darned if I know"
9. Louise's partner
10. Architect with an avian name
12. All talk, no action
14. A type of football kick
15. Banal writer
16. Roller derby wear
19. Planet's icy area
20. Sydney salutation
21. Single guy's home

DOWN

1. Metaphor for a thorough search
2. Leave alone
3. Soft touch
4. Far from here
5. Kids' racers
6. Kid's sidewalk business
11. Admire
13. Antiquated
17. Get dressed
18. Where Wile E. gets his gadgets

Answers on page 183.

X MARKS THE SPOT

ACROSS

1. Release
5. Camera lens setting
8. Goes up and down
9. Final consumer
10. Athlete's thirst quencher
11. Become ragged
13. Trade center
16. "Confess!"
17. Elicit
20. Carrier making short hops
21. All together, in music
22. Automotive dud
23. Barely beat

DOWN

1. Birds do it
2. "Have a bite!"
3. Picket line phrase
4. Military practice
5. Become harder to see
6. Dress rehearsal
7. Bright and bouncy
12. Frustrating series of calls
14. Crude container
15. Accept blame quietly
16. Batting game for kids
18. "A Tale ____ Cities"
19. Advise of danger

Answers on page 183.

COMMON PHRASES

ACROSS

1. Small agricultural enterprise
5. McCartney's instrument
8. Cultural no-no
9. "Shouldn't have done that!"
11. Approve automatically
13. Along with the rest
14. Totally swamp
17. Continuously
20. Tapped into, as a resource
21. "I respectfully disagree"
22. Too curious
23. Help vacationing neighbors

DOWN

1. Boy-meets-girl event
2. Grapefruit choice
3. Armchair quarterback, for one
4. Money in Moscow
6. Island greeting
7. Get rid of, as a hangover
10. Basic guidelines
12. Gave to the teacher
15. "Odyssey" hero
16. Crude shed
18. Age measurement
19. "Aw shucks!"

Answers on page 183.

JOBS AND INDUSTRIES

ACROSS

1. Martha or Rod
5. First Greek letter
8. Detectives
9. "... silk purse out of a sow's ___"
10. They're equal and opposite
12. "___ Gets Drafted" (1942 Disney cartoon)
13. "Duck!" and "Timber!"
15. "Great" Macedonian king
16. Balloon-breaking sound
18. Hollywood's business
20. "Days of Our Lives" setting
21. Sheaths, shifts, jumpers

DOWN

1. "Chattanooga Shoe ___ Boy"
2. Ecological
3. Land of the wallaby
4. "Made in ___"
5. "___ approved" (hotel sign)
6. Focus group?
7. "A" on box scores
11. Freedom from bigotry
12. Some casino staff
14. "Early Sunday Morning" artist Hopper
17. Deer trails, maybe
19. Truck make

Answers on page 183.

A GLITZY LIFESTYLE

ACROSS

1. Down the quarterback
3. Light and filmy
9. Curly lock
10. Clamor
11. Luxury in some homes
13. Sheriffs and marshals
15. French eatery
17. Deep sorrow or anguish
19. Big payoff game
20. Cocktail for 007
21. Euclid's subject
22. Go steady with

DOWN

1. Fall behind
2. Craft for Hiawatha
4. One-up with smarts
5. PR agents, often
6. Nickname for a handy guy
7. Asian food staple
8. Dapper Dan
12. Precipitous plunge
14. "Good job!"
16. Mallet
18. "The Good Earth" locale
19. Huey or Howie

Answers on page 184.

STORIES AND SAYINGS

ACROSS

1. Sanctuaries
5. "Kaboom!"
8. Atlanta's Omni e.g.
9. Watches someone else's kitties, perhaps
10. Inspirational tale
11. Jam or pickle
12. Dish the dirt
15. "Holy cow!", to Annie
19. Easily stretched
20. Dens
21. Crawl or swarm
22. "Maltese Falcon" writer

DOWN

1. Flag support
2. Shades, e.g.
3. Country singer's quality
4. Jurassic Park critter
6. Baja buddy
7. Dress in one's Sunday best
11. Notably significant
13. Conjecture
14. O'Hara's "My Friend ___"
16. Colorful playing marble
17. Nothing, slangily
18. Fiber used in rug-making

Answers on page 184.

EVOCATIVE PHRASES

ACROSS

1. Gives a little leeway
8. Ballpark nibbles
9. "Snowy" marsh bird
10. Auto gear
11. Bird that lays the largest eggs
12. Carroll's "Mad" tea drinker
13. Server on skates, in the '60s
16. Christmas-pageant trio
18. Accumulate, as wealth
20. Olympic speed skater Ohno
21. Hard to pin down
22. Feeling before entering a haunted house, maybe

DOWN

1. Arrow-shooting cherub
2. Hopper in depression? No, a British sausage dish
3. Sleep, informally
4. Army mule, for one
5. Bloodhound's clue
6. It might help keep you out of jail
7. Whopper topper
12. Relaxing soak
14. Generally speaking
15. Nightclub or bar mitzvah feature
17. Garlicky mayo
19. Slow cooker dishes

Answers on page 184.

SOME OF THE BEST PICTURES

ACROSS

1. Best picture of 1992
7. Dairy case items
8. Beat, as the heart
10. Vital carrier
11. Island of a 1945 battle
12. Current government
14. Submarine sandwich
17. Home for fighter jets
19. Nouveau ___
21. "Sunny" egg parts
22. Prying tool
23. Best picture of 1943

DOWN

1. Felix of "The Odd Couple"
2. Pistol or rifle
3. Enter quickly
4. Performance preceder
5. Loop for a lobe
6. Best picture of 1964
9. Best picture of 1990
13. Big ape
15. Thornton Wilder play
16. Tentatively schedule, with "in"
18. On a cruise, say
20. Deadly snake

Answers on page 184.

RHYME TIME 2

ACROSS

1. "Call My Name" jazz singer James
5. "Judge not, ___ ye be judged"
9. Angle or athlete prefix
12. "Ahab the ___" (Ray Stevens song)
13. City west of Salt Lake on I-80
14. Accelerate sharply
15. Calls at poker
16. Its symbol is five rings
18. Burping in public, e.g.
20. Carpet calculations
21. First five Bible books
23. Edmonton players
26. Bucker under a buckaroo
28. "Behold," to Caesar
29. Egg ___ Yung
32. Feed, as a furnace
34. Arm art, for short
35. Badgers for payment
37. Kind of conference
39. Common theater name
41. Tarnish, as a reputation
44. Brown-bag contents
46. Arctic Eskimo
48. Jeep SUV
51. "Uncle Remus" character ___ Rabbit
52. Knack for melody
53. Darjeeling and oolong

54. 30% of the world's land
55. Bit of food
56. Exist, in France
57. "... which nobody can ___!"

DOWN

1. 90 degrees right of north
2. Cover the tab
3. Cardio-boxing regimen
4. Engross wholly
5. Author Tolstoy
6. "Enchanted" film girl
7. Shoot up abruptly
8. "My Cousin Vinnie" Oscar winner
9. Cut into thirds
10. Family room, familiarly
11. Drips in an ICU
17. "___ Rider" (Eastwood movie)
19. Rowboat gear
22. Microwaveable turnover
24. Indianapolis's ___ Dome
25. Prepare, as a table
27. Fish ___ fowl
29. 32nd pres.
30. French affirmative
31. Poised for trouble
33. "La Bamba" star Morales
36. Defamatory remark

108

38. "Arabian Nights" sailor

40. Fed. bond

42. "Grey's Anatomy" extra

43. Link

45. Catch wind of

47. Airline seat feature

48. Big boss

49. Belly laugh syllable

50. "Brooklyn" or "Vietnam" ending

1	2	3	4		5	6	7	8		9	10	11
12					13					14		
15					16			17				
18			19		20							
	21			22		23			24	25
		26		27			28			
29	30	31		32			33		34		
35			36		37			38			
39				40		41			42	43	
		44			45		46			47
48	49					50		51			
52				53				54			
55				56				57			

Answers on page 185.

HE WROTE THE SONGS

ACROSS

1. "I Write the Songs" singer
8. Instrumental blather
9. Brewed drink for teetotalers
10. "No problem!"
12. Potato bump
13. #1 hit of 1974 by 1-Across
15. With 24-Across, #1 hit of 1976 by 1-Across
17. Tackle a slope
18. Very narrow boundary
21. Swellhead's journey?
23. Banishment
24. With 15-Across #1 hit of 1976 by 1-Across

DOWN

1. Flops at the box office
2. Blade holder
3. 1958 #1 song about talking back
4. "I was elsewhere" excuses
5. "Now ___ seen everything!"
6. In high gear
7. Hole wheat bread?
11. Prosperous period
13. Potato option
14. Kenya's capital
16. Cute smile feature
19. Shot from a tee
20. Throw out
22. Kind of whiskey

Answers on page 185.

OXYMORONS

ACROSS

3. They feuded with the McCoys
7. Annual book of facts
8. Bricks that snap together
9. With 10-Across, "big-little" oxymoron
10. See 9-Across
12. Sly and inventive
14. Lake ___ (source of the Mississippi)
16. With 18-Across, "unarranged arrangement" oxymoron
18. See 16-Across
21. Civil wrongs
22. Messed up
23. Hoodwink

DOWN

1. Pancake
2. Peg Bundy or Marge Simpson
3. Place to loiter with pals
4. Hammock occupant
5. Peas, beans, etc.
6. Backtalk
11. Newfoundland neighbor
13. "Ocean," to "canoe"
15. Defeat easily
17. Mirror-ball dance genre
19. Barbie and Raggedy Ann
20. Ticket leftover

Answers on page 185.

CHARACTERS AND PHRASES

ACROSS

1. Rustic film couple of "The Egg and I"
7. Workaday grind
8. Border collie's flock
9. "Humble" home
10. Trees favored by giraffes
11. Birds often made in origami
13. Desert succulent
16. Impressive and then some
17. Fiery gemstones
20. Former Swedish imports
21. Beach near Diamond Head
22. Be kept waiting

DOWN

1. "The Sound of Music" lady
2. Animated canine or Houston ballplayer
3. Sharpshooter
4. Moniker for Tarzan
5. "Cats" poet
6. Brings to light
11. Great work of literature
12. In days of yore
14. Eradicate
15. Baseball great Reese
18. Licorice-flavored herb
19. Clipper features

Answers on page 185.

LEADING MEN

ACROSS

1. Fancy neckwear
7. Certain NFL linemen
10. Broken rock used in foundations
11. Fury or anger
12. Cool star of "Cool Hand Luke," 1967
14. Playground retort to "Are not!"
15. Bligh and Queeg, e.g.
16. Fishing and hunting guide in Scotland
17. "Captain Blood" star, 1938
21. Decorative table with three legs
22. Handbell ringer of old
23. Former Israeli leader Golda
27. "Grapes of Wrath" star, 1940
29. Brian who produced U2
30. By a whisker
31. Amtrak stop: abbr.
32. Course after the salad

DOWN

1. Harp, in Italy
2. "The King and I" kingdom
3. PC brains
4. Column base
5. Camel hair color
6. Make explicit
7. In a weak way
8. Au ___ (with bread crumbs)
9. Early breath freshener
13. Handball playing surface
16. "Hallelujah!"
17. Cuts into glass
18. Get again, as a video
19. Spoil, as a parade
20. Letters above 0, on the phone
23. Comedian Sahl
24. Cabinet dept. with an oil rig on its seal abbr.
25. Empty, as threats
26. Funny Martha of old TV
28. Season ticket holder

1	2	3	4	5	6	■	7	8	9
10						■	11		
12					13				
14				■	15				
■	■	■	■	16					
17	18	19	20						
21						■	■	■	■
22					■	23	24	25	26
27				28					
29			■	30					
31			■	32					

117

Answers on page 186.

BROADWAY MUSICALS

ACROSS

1. 10th grader, for short
5. "Dracula" portrayer Lugosi
9. ___ podrida (Spanish stew)
10. Have too much of, for short
11. Actor Lukas of "Witness"
12. ___'clock (end of lunch break)
13. 1944 Broadway musical about three sailors on leave
15. Himalayan goat
16. Get in the crosshairs
19. Former Pan Am rival
22. 1947 Broadway hit about a mysterious Scottish village
24. "Silent" president Coolidge
25. Candy man played by Depp
26. Bishop's path, in chess: abbr.
28. 1964 Broadway musical with Barbra Streisand
33. God of war
34. "Milk's Favorite Cookie"
35. Carpenter's clamp
36. Like average folks, in Britain
37. Aide-de-camp, briefly
38. "The Chalk Garden" author Bagnold

DOWN

1. Area near Greenwich Village
2. "The Good Earth" heroine
3. Subdivision map
4. # in a tweet
5. Cozy diner seat
6. Classic Art Carney role
7. MGM co-founder Marcus
8. "Author unknown" byline
14. Erode
16. "Dancing With the Stars" network
17. "I Got Rhythm" lyricist Gershwin
18. Gentle quality
20. Stir-fry pan
21. Actress Ortiz of "Ugly Betty"
23. Confounded
27. Atlas closeup
28. Hannibal Lecter's bean of choice
29. "Exodus" author Leon
30. Clothes unwrinkler
31. "The Labors of Hercules" painter Guido
32. Like heavy metal concerts

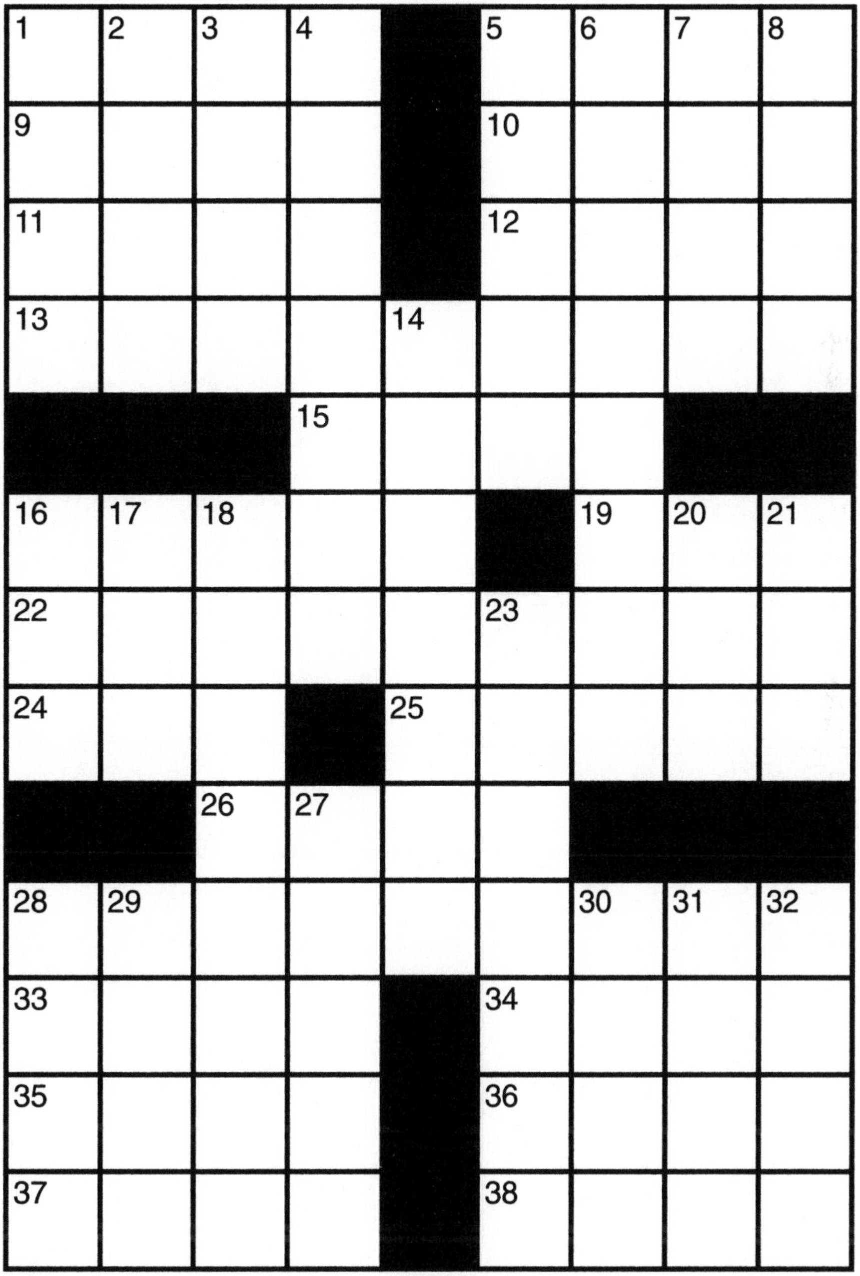

Answers on page 186.

HOW TO TAKE CHARGE

ACROSS

1. "A Fish Called ___"
6. Frozen drip
12. Kill the exam, slangily
13. Pay a visit to
14. Take charge in the henhouse?
16. Base eatery
17. Golf course peg
18. Have a bite
19. Electric-fan sound
20. Take charge at the immunization clinic?
25. Harem rooms
26. Brit's bathroom
27. Cambodian leader Lon ___
28. Old-fashioned letter opener
33. Take charge in a horse race?
35. Capital of Montana
36. "The Destroyer," in Hinduism
37. Some mattresses
38. Carved Native American pole

DOWN

1. Less than hot
2. Missed ___: blew one's entrance
3. "Little House on the Prairie" character ___ Oleson
4. Many truck engines
5. To boot
6. Bjork's country: abbr.
7. Poet Sandburg
8. UN agcy. that won the 1969 Nobel Peace Prize
9. Fate who spins the thread of life
10. Come unglued
11. Comes in
15. "What ___ God wrought"
19. Directory of notables
20. Spiral shells
21. Old-time actress Renee
22. Fingers-in-ears sounds
23. "In the Valley of ___" (2007 Tommy Lee Jones film)
24. Like the worst loser
28. Big Apple fashion inits.
29. Airport arr. estimates
30. "___ the jackpot!"
31. Paris's ___ Gauche
32. Unsolicited e-mail
34. Disney film frame

Answers on page 186.

COMMON PHRASES

ACROSS

1. Rustic pipe
5. Clear as a bell
8. Sort of
9. Guard at a post
10. Elaborate dinner
12. "Aloha," in Israel
13. "The Foundation Trilogy" author
17. Apt anagram for Bart
19. "Quiet!"
20. Impending danger, proverbially
21. Greet casually
22. Act of sedition

DOWN

1. Auto body
2. Dome-topped building
3. Passageway
4. Self-serve meal
6. Baked-potato garnish
7. Like London fogs
11. So to speak
14. Genghis Khan's followers
15. Ex-soldier
16. Finger-wagging words
17. Cereal holders
18. Calm, as fears

Answers on page 186.

TOM HANKS MOVIES

ACROSS

1. Tom Hanks starred with Meryl Streep in 2017's "The ___"
5. ... playing legendary newspaperman ___ Bradlee
8. Allied jumping-off point of July 1944
12. "Cleopatra" river
13. "Hips Don't ___" (2006 Shakira hit)
14. "Hawaii Five-o" star Scott
15. Op-ed artist Pat known for caricatures
17. Comes to the rescue
18. Love letter salutation
19. In a 2016 movie, Hanks touched down successfully as the heroic pilot called "___"
21. Barnyard mama
22. Employs
23. Bunk, e.g.
26. Popular deal-of-the-day website
29. Hanks was New York lawyer James Donovan in this 2015 historical drama
33. Court precedent
34. Rifleman's org.
35. Casual conversation
36. Purely or simply: abbr.
39. Hanks starred with Halle Berry in 2012's science fiction epic, "___ Atlas"
40. Hanks was Eamon ___ in the techno-thriller "The Circle," 2017
44. "Cape ___" (1991 De Niro film)

45. Shapeless
47. 40–30 tennis score, maybe
48. Big name in home dyes
49. "The ___ King" (2019 remake starring Beyoncé)
50. Blue staters, for short
51. Last letter of the Hebrew alphabet, similar to the letter T
52. "Raggedy" dolls

DOWN

1. ___ Penh, Cambodia (Var.)
2. Like a grease monkey's rag
3. Arrived safely under the throw
4. Cheyenne shelter
5. Loud sound from trumpets
6. "Ich Bin ___ Berliner": JFK
7. Browse the web
8. Increase proportionately
9. Out-of-control drop
10. "Luck Be a ___"
11. Add-___ (annexes)
16. "Turn left" command
20. GI hangouts
23. "Dr. Who" network
24. Slice of history
25. Deny
26. Pai ___ (Chinese gambling game)

27. "... ___ the fields we go..."

28. Clandestine govt. org.

30. Renders harmless, as a bull

31. Actress Summer of "Firefly"

32. Humbly accept blame

36. "Dancing With the Stars" network

37. Dit's counterpart

38. Cello's smaller cousin

39. Formally hand over

41. Sprawled

42. Bond's alma mater

43. Deep desires

44. "In" thing, for now

46. "My Big Fat Greek Wedding" star Vardalos

Answers on page 187.

GOOD SHOWS

ACROSS

1. Buccaneer's Bay
6. Expire, as a subscription
11. College founder Yale
12. ___-ski party
13. 1964 musical fantasy film with Julie Andrews and Dick Van Dyke
15. Major of many a poli sci student
16. Comstock's famous find
17. "Singin' in the Rain" girl
19. TV's ___ Tin Tin
20. 1975 musical about Broadway dancers
24. Fed. watchdog agency
25. Animal protection org.
26. Regarding, in memos
28. Computer whiz, slangily
32. 1995 Disney film set in Africa but influenced by Hamlet
34. Beauty of Troy
35. "The Gondoliers" flower girl
36. Part of PGA: abbr.
37. Church council

DOWN

1. Fill-in worker, briefly
2. Apple spray withdrawn in 1989
3. Get stuck in mud
4. Dough used in spanakopita
5. Nannies
6. Once around the track
7. GE stove or fridge
8. A ___ (assumed true)
9. Submit, as an application
10. Ancient Palestinian
14. Openly admit
18. Mountaineering feats
20. Christie of mystery
21. Redeems one's chips, with "in"
22. Monopoly buys
23. Subservient sort
27. Butter alternative
29. Word on a backwoods towel?
30. Not ___ many words
31. "Gadzooks!" relative
33. Entrepreneur's mag.

Answers on page 187.

BACK-TO-BACK VICTORIES

ACROSS

1. Doles out
8. Mind a youngster
9. Upright, for one
10. Alternative to pajamas
12. Be drowsy
14. "Emergency!"
16. "I give in!"
17. WWII president
19. Sniff out
20. Beat-up cars
23. "King Kong" star Watts
24. Tennis shots
25. They look at screens

DOWN

1. Arab emirate
2. Italian volcano
3. T-bill payout
4. Wine tastes
5. Post-season game
6. Kicks around
7. Handle difficulties
11. Do a great job
13. "Moby Dick" author
15. Exit
18. Face down temptation
19. What the Titanic did
21. Board chairs, e.g.
22. Capital of Ukraine
24. Letter repeated back-to-back in four answers

Answers on page 187.

DOUBLE VISION

ACROSS

1. "That sounds about right"
4. Black-tie blowout
8. Talk radio source, often
9. Hamburger topper
11. Vibrating vocal effect
12. Earrings or socks, perhaps
14. Art of folding paper
16. "Caribbean Queen" singer Billy
18. "Days of Our Lives," for one
19. Tart flavor
20. Flip-flops or setbacks

DOWN

1. Its license plates say "Famous Potatoes"
2. Steadfast
3. Look-alike, as in 12-Across
5. Goddess of love and beauty
6. White-knuckled
7. "Bury My Heart at Wounded ___"
10. Hunch or sixth sense
12. Like a romantic evening, maybe
13. Make a pitch for a hitch
15. Plus which
17. Comes closer

Answers on page 187.

PARASITE

ACROSS

1. Pitcher plant victim
4. "Parasite" director, producer, and writer: ___ Joon-ho
8. Share some gossip
12. Hawaii's Mauna ___ volcano
13. Flyer to Tel Aviv
14. It means "commander" in Arabic
15. Game lover's purchase
16. Dynamic opener
17. Omar of "House"
18. "Parasite" was Oscar's ___ of 2019
21. Female enlistee in WWII
22. What permissive parents may choose to spare
25. "Faust" character
28. Vets-to-be
29. Number of Disney Dalmatians
30. Pizza joint appliance
31. Party with power
32. Give a long look
33. Beyond the horizon
34. And the rest, briefly
35. Where van Gogh painted "The Night Cafe"
36. Philadelphia hockey team
38. New Deal agcy. of 1933
39. "Parasite" won four major Oscars, including one for "Best International ___"

44. Ump's ruling
46. Campsite visitor
47. Take-home item
48. Type of bond, for short
49. Slangy turnarounds
50. Colony member
51. Arcade game ___-Ball
52. State of comfort
53. Dit's counterpart in Morse code

DOWN

1. Toning target
2. Wolf's gait
3. Barks sharply
4. "Help me out here, bud"
5. Olive oil's ___ acid
6. Sting figure
7. Opening between the vocal cords
8. Big name in tractors and such
9. Bygone Chrysler
10. Drink sample
11. Slugger's stat
19. Sealy choice
20. Nervous speaker's sounds
23. Leak out slowly
24. Breaks down
25. Tip, as one's derby
26. Feedback for a prof.

27. Nearly mint, to a collector
28. Big chain in health supplements
31. "I'm not making it up!"
32. Rival of Seles
34. The Mesozoic, e.g.
35. Reluctant
37. Causing chills, maybe

38. They beat twos
40. Iris container
41. Apple store purchase
42. Clark's crush
43. Legend
44. Most NPR stations
45. Puffin, e.g.

Answers on page 188.

MIDDLE-NAME STARS

ACROSS

1. Castle barrier
5. Fishhook features
10. Nick Charles's dog
11. Basketball Hall of Famer Thomas
12. "Gone With the Wind" star whose first name was William
14. ___ voce (in a low voice)
15. Brazil's soccer star
16. Gallery hangings
18. Chihuahua of '90s cartoons
19. "The Social Network" actress whose first name is Patricia
23. Stomach acid, to a chemist
24. Simile's center
25. Company that owns elevator.com
27. Chilling, as champagne
31. "The Pink Panther" star whose first name was James
33. Perrier rival
34. Country singer k. d. ___
35. Not very reputable
36. Social insects

DOWN

1. Non-P.C. choices?
2. Capitol on a fjord
3. Rat-___ (gun sound)
4. Clan pattern
5. Word before Ben or Dipper
6. "Chop-chop!" in a memo
7. "Immaculate Conception" artist Jose de ___
8. Tool for melons
9. Jungle queen of comics
13. State divided in 1945
17. Cicely of "Roots"
19. Colossus island
20. Eight-note interval
21. Wilde of TV's "House"
22. Philippines capital
26. Thailand's former name
28. Lendl or Pavlov
29. "Indian-head" item
30. Many MIT grads abbr.
32. Letters after Sen. Charles Schumer's name

1	2	3	4		5	6	7	8	9
10					11				
12				13					
14						15			
			16		17		18		
19	20	21				22			
23				24					
25			26		27		28	29	30
31				32					
33						34			
35						36			

135

IN A RUSH

ACROSS

1. Jealous to the max
8. "There ___ to be a law!"
9. Small suitcases
10. University of Wyoming city
11. Grand-scale stories
12. "Voila!"
13. The ego and id are part of it
16. A companion of Porthos
18. Reykjavik's country
20. "I'd rather not discuss it"
21. Chubby Checker's dance
22. Church, mosque or temple

DOWN

1. Halloween spook
2. "Prepare to fence!"
3. "Hurry!"
4. Visible
5. Every which way
6. American of Japanese heritage
7. "Got it"
12. Modeling clay for moppets
14. Telethon's beneficiary
15. So done with
17. Like most people in India
19. Prevent or discourage

Answers on page 188.

THREE 45S

ACROSS

1. 45
8. Replay option
9. Mood music genre
10. With 14-Across, '45
11. Dry, as wine
12. Parting words
14. See 10-Across
17. Pro-prohibition
18. Baton-passing event
20. "Amen, brother!"
21. Map collection
23. .45

DOWN

1. Roast beef au _____
2. Like an open secret
3. Unauthorized DVD
4. Checked for fractures, perhaps
5. Smoldering fragment
6. Took care of
7. Private investigator
10. Class outing
13. Birds do it
15. Outfielder's catch
16. Health facility
18. Nostalgic fashion trend
19. Speak off the cuff
22. What to call an officer

Answers on page 188.

APPLE CORE

ACROSS

1. Loudly delicious
7. Ingredients for ice cream splits
8. "Outta sight!"
9. Court org.
10. Decisive
12. Lent prelude
17. Put up with
20. Scene of "Miss Saigon," briefly
21. Kind of bar
22. Place to secure a boat
23. Long isthmus divider

DOWN

1. Reach of the law
2. Sudden fright
3. Doubtfire's title
4. Horseman?
5. First words of "Satisfaction"
6. Oscar of "Sesame Street," e.g.
7. S&L, e.g.
11. Kind of whiskey
13. Seeing things as they are
14. Daytime timer
15. Consumes entirely
16. Pollution haze
18. Bean of old game shows
19. Render inaudible, with "out"
22. Word for apple at the center of 4 answers in this puzzle

Answers on page 189.

GRANDMA'S PANTRY

ACROSS

1. Leveling wedge
5. Copy of a mag.
8. Big ___
12. Animal rights org.
13. Reggae relative
14. Dutch treat
15. Strong plow pullers
16. See-through data: abbr.
17. Sand hill
18. Orange spread
21. Indian holiday destination
22. ___ Brynner, actor
24. Multi ___, like cut gems
28. Excite: 2 wds.
31. Computer port
32. Abner's radio friend
34. Go astray
35. Place: Latin
38. Pulpy refuse in sugar-making
41. Resume, for short
43. Ammo unit: abbr.
45. Candied fruit
48. Greek portico
50. US secretive org.
51. Boost: abbr.
53. Estonian or Latvian
54. Architects' org.
55. Arm of the Black Sea
56. Loony
57. "Bad" cholesterol
58. Musical mark

DOWN

1. Sugar quantity in recipes
2. Witch's curse
3. News bit
4. Cope
5. "Moby-Dick" narrator
6. Gull-like bird
7. Unfortunately
8. Interfere
9. Musical direction
10. ___-of-war, battleship
11. Final word
19. Decompose
20. Arctic diver
23. Dogcatcher's cargo
25. Starting from: 2 wds.
26. North-of-the-border network
27. Nickname
29. Cry of success
30. Can for future use
33. ___ law
36. Nazi submarines: 2 wds.
37. One of the sixty in an h.
39. Safari sight
40. Rocky Balboa's Love
42. Garbage

44. Book ID: abbr.
45. Wild West revolver
46. Bibliographical abbr.

47. ____ Ferrari, auto designer
49. Kind of cross
52. Simple sack

1	2	3	4		5	6	7		8	9	10	11
12					13				14			
15					16				17			
		18		19			20					
			21				22				23	
24	25	26				27		28		29		30
31					32		33			34		
35			36	37		38		39	40			
			41		42		43					
44		45				46				47		
48	49				50				51		52	
53					54				55			
56					57				58			

Answers on page 189.

APT ANAGRAMS

ACROSS

1. "New Yorker" cartoonist Peter
5. Carpet with thick pile
9. 1987 Best Actress for "Moonstruck"
10. "Return of the Jedi" princess
11. Apt anagram of BAD CREDIT?
13. Dog breed kept at Buckingham Palace
14. "What's the ___?" ("Who cares?")
15. Dutch river or beer
17. Apt anagram of DIRTY ROOM?
20. New York city famous for silverware
21. FDR home loan org.
22. "Boyhood" star Hawke
26. Apt anagram of SO I'M CUTER?
28. Campbell of country music
29. Cleveland's Great Lake
30. Mathematical chances
31. "___ in the Clowns"

DOWN

1. Band with a lightning bolt in its logo
2. Prefix for stat
3. Cornhusker State: Abbr.
4. Japanese paper-folding art
5. Beehive State capital initials
6. Move in the direction of
7. More breezy
8. Persistent pest
12. More shy and hesitant
16. Sculpture garden figures
17. "Please stay!"
18. Waiting for tech support, often
19. Cleaned out, as with a pipe cleaner
23. Add to the staff
24. Z ___ zebra
25. Crave
27. Brain and spinal cord, initially

Answers on page 189.

HELLO, AUSSIES

ACROSS

1. Casino receipts
5. Wide gap in type
12. "Survivor" immunity token
13. Egg-laying mammal
14. Blue, in Berlin
15. Christmas tree decoration
16. Indigenous word for a creek that runs during the rainy season only
18. "La ___" (Debussy piece)
19. Agcy. that aids start-ups
20. "Beg pardon!"
21. It might give you a jump-start
22. Freezing prefix
23. Cranky
25. "Golden Boy" dramatist Clifford
27. Clasp hands
28. ___ Lumpur, Malaysian capital
29. Electric fan sound
30. Dune buggy, e.g.
31. Pate de ___ gras
32. 911 call responder
35. A grand slam home run gets four
36. Where "G'day!" is heard
38. Satchel for guys
40. Abbr. on egg cartons
41. Stressed
42. Be alive with
43. "The Simpsons" principal
44. ___ on the wrist

DOWN

1. "They Call Me MISTER ___!" (1970 film)
2. "Whose Line Is It Anyway?" feature
3. Adorable Australian
4. Month preceding Rosh Hashanah
5. Cheap cigar, slangily
6. Grauman's Chinese Theatre, formerly ___
7. All-male bash
8. Poe's "The Narrative of Arthur Gordon ___"
9. Part of a gorilla costume
10. Wedge-shaped
11. Lost sheep, to a lawyer
13. Mardi Gras sandwiches, informally
17. Artery from the heart
22. "Simpsons" frame
23. President who resigned during the fall of Saigon
24. A missing pencil may be behind one
25. Australian wilderness
26. Dan Brown's "The ___ Code"
27. Polished, as shoes
28. Destinies, to some
29. Humdinger
31. Strong suit

146

32. '50s four-wheeled flop

33. Euripides play

34. "Little" Chaplin role

36. Nora of "SNL"

37. Cashews or filberts

39. Autograph-seeker's need

Answers on page 189.

PEOPLE AND PLACES

ACROSS

7. "Deadwood" territory
8. Banded marbles
9. "Twas on the ___ of Capri..."
10. Lab sample for testing
11. "Peekaboo" follower
13. Innocents
15. Tub passenger of rhyme
17. Trumpets and tubas
20. Idaho nickname
21. " Not to mention..."
23. Act the rat
24. Alarms

DOWN

1. Bases, in baseball slang
2. Candy heart line
3. Grandfather, in "Peter and the Wolf"
4. Polished, as a car
5. Boat harbor
6. Look like
12. Key used between words
14. "Green Eggs and Ham" author
16. Bogus
18. Beetle in Egyptian carvings
19. "10,000 ___" (Minnesota license plate slogan)
22. Acorn, essentially

Answers on page 190.

ETHAN ALLEN'S DICTIONARY

ACROSS

1. Cantina order
4. With 8-Across, giving up just a little?
8. See 4-Across
10. Letters of debt
11. In shock
12. Eccentric sort
13. Cold spike
15. With 18-Across, elegant renaissance?
18. See 15-Across
21. Asimov's genre
23. "Fingers crossed!"
24. With 25-Across, on-topic animal keeper?
25. See 24-Across
26. Reply to roll call

DOWN

1. Stuck together
2. Whirlpool bath brand
3. Classic car
5. Tip over
6. "Open sesame!" sayer
7. Measure up to
9. Object of fan adoration
13. Reduced to rubble
14. Engineered simply
16. Choir platform
17. Allegedly harmful look
19. Nary a soul
20. Pub offering
22. PR concern

Answers on page 190.

MAPS AND LOCATIONS

ACROSS

1. Their suits come with briefs
4. Amethyst or turquoise
7. "___ obliged!"
8. Rival of Lincoln
9. Baghdad native
11. T ___ tango
13. Google, say
14. Morning mugful
17. Chore list header
19. Absorber of UV rays
22. Take out of commission
23. It's not pretty
24. Blog comments
25. On paper

DOWN

1. Highway posting
2. Kansas's largest city
3. Radio crackling
4. "The Shawshank Redemption" setting
5. "The Island of Doctor Moreau" writer
6. Hunter's need
10. Brow shape
12. Bull's-eye, for Target
13. Web surfer's guide
15. Semi's load
16. Like a jack-o'-lantern
18. Egypt leads the world in their production
20. Check for fit
21. Ancient Egyptians revered it

Answers on page 190.

ACROSS

1. Bread fit for gyros
5. "Minnesota" pool pro
9. Bug for payment
12. "Right on, preacher"
13. Arches National Park state
14. "Now __ heard everything!"
15. Give an edge to
16. "Cubic" Rubik
17. Aral or Caspian
18. After losing everything in the recession, Fern (Frances McDormand) joins real-life nomads exploring the American West in this 2020 film
20. Bit of butter
21. Aides for MDs
22. Classic Icelandic poetry
24. Animal support org.
27. Response to "Would I look good in this?"
30. Act as usher
31. "Masterpiece" airer
32. Bad marks for a teen
33. Not kidding
35. High priest's garment
36. Eight, to Hans und Franz
37. "Right, skipper"
38. It's not much

40. McDormand won a Best Actress Oscar for her portrayal of Minnesota police chief Marge __ in 1996's "Fargo"
45. "Boola Boola" collegian
46. Foil's duller relative
47. Cloud of gloom
48. "Gilligan's Island" signal
49. "And others," briefly
50. Busy doing nothing
51. Spot for a first shot
52. "J'accuse" author Emile
53. Cheek by jowl

DOWN

1. Chess "soldier"
2. "As I see it" online
3. Abound
4. South Pole region
5. Coal and oil, for two
6. Old Gillette razor model
7. Hide workers
8. Of inferior quality
9. McDormand is a journalist profiling student revolutionaries in this 2021 film, "The French __"
10. Colorful eye part
11. Like Felix, but not Oscar
19. "The Double Helix" subject
23. It's not needed with Huggies

24. "Kick-___" (2010 superhero movie)

25. "Catch my drift?"

26. McDormand plays the brash Dr. Verstak in 1997's fact-based Australian war film, "___ Road"

27. "The Superstation"

28. Tokyo-born Grammy winner

29. "Deliverance" actor Beatty

31. Encouraged in mischief

34. "That's awkward"

35. Aperture of a needle

37. "A Passage to India" woman ___ Quested

38. Audition, for instance

39. Soothing botanical

41. "Hud" Oscar-winner Patricia

42. "Smooth Operator" singer

43. Big earthenware jar

44. Brave or Giant, slangily

1	2	3	4	■	5	6	7	8	■	9	10	11
12				■	13				■	14		
15				■	16				■	17		
18			19						■	20		
■	■	■	21			■	22		23		■	■
24	25	26			■	27					28	29
30				■	31			■	32			
33			34			■	35					
■	■	36				■	37			■	■	■
38	39		■	40		41				42	43	44
45			■	46				■	47			
48			■	49				■	50			
51			■	52				■	53			

Answers on page 190.

FUN & GAMES

Across

1. Check the bar code
5. Family chart
9. Blog entries
14. Teeny bit
15. Jazz great Hines
16. Mr. T's TV outfit
17. Deanna of "Star Trek: TNG"
18. Landers and Meara
19. Conk out, as a car
20. It has its ups and downs (No. 1)
23. Blown up, as a neg.
24. Arson evidence
25. FedEx arrival
28. These can be checkered
30. Jump causer
32. Backyard storage facility
33. Craven who directed "Swamp Thing"
35. "___ be in England": Browning
37. Butterworth or Doubtfire
38. It has its ups and downs (No. 2)
41. Pie-mode link
43. Knit's partner
44. Cpl. or Sgt.
45. Mazar of "GoodFellas"
47. Co. now part of Verizon
48. Carousel figure
52. Big rig fuel
54. Dish of roasted roots
56. Caboose's place
57. It has its ups and downs (No. 3)
61. Squeezed (out), as wet towels
63. Juice, so to speak: Abbr.
64. Bear whose porridge was too hot
65. Midler or Davis
66. Activist Parks
67. Novello of old films
68. Pacific salmon varieties
69. One in arrears
70. Put in the mail

Down

1. Military status account, briefly
2. Popular Mexican beer
3. Coral rings
4. Clip-and-file item
5. Salty drops
6. Cowboy's dressing?
7. Cube inventor Rubik
8. "Born Free" lioness
9. Linguini, for one
10. Frisky swimmers
11. "I haven't a clue"
12. Chess champion Mikhail
13. Opposite of lge.
21. Cut some slack
22. Exact, to a Brit
26. Always, in a poem
27. Joseph Smith's denom.
29. Snake-eyes number

30. "I Dreamed a Dream" singer Susan
31. Cry from one who just got the joke
34. Baby carrier brand
36. Boo-boo
38. Slugger of 714 homers
39. Old PC screen
40. "Barney Miller" actor Jack
41. Sum up
42. Island neckwear
46. Really enjoys
49. Make a backup copy, say

50. Easily attached accessory
51. R. Murrow or G. Robinson
53. Slight advantages
54. Bel ___ (Italian cheese)
55. Felix's "odd" friend
58. Fictional detective Wolfe
59. Gentle firelight, e.g.
60. Not Meth. or Presby.
61. Pugilist's org.
62. Bygone Olds

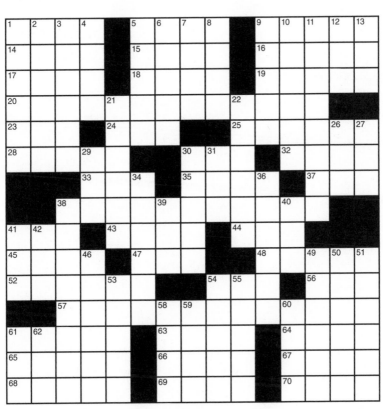

Answers on page 191.

MISHMASH

ACROSS

1. Follower of Jason
5. Blows away, in a way
8. European neolithic monument
10. Topple
11. Everglades makeup
13. Safe harbors
15. Ouzo flavoring
18. Kind of mint or speaker
19. Captain Kidd's haul, e.g.
20. Like Eastwood in three Leone films

DOWN

1. "Sour grapes" fabulist
2. Garden figure
3. Type of embroidery
4. Matchless
6. Sweet-talk
7. Greets the general
9. One who must be above suspicion, in a saying
11. South Pacific islanders
12. "The ___ Honeymoon," 1914 song
14. "But will it play in ___?"
16. Birch bark craft
17. Livestock shelters

Answers on page 191.

RHYME TIME 3

ACROSS

1. Bottle stopper
5. "Antiques Roadshow" network
8. Funny comment
12. Black or fire gem
13. Microbrew choice
14. Abbr. on a meat stamp
15. Like certain battery terminals
17. Hard to grab hold of
18. Game of subterfuge
20. '90s jet, now retired
21. "Seeing red" feeling
22. Developer's land
25. Wee colonist
26. "Include me ___": Sam Goldwyn
29. Like a wedding anniversary forgetter
32. Chin or Siam ending
33. "The Fresh Prince of ___ Air"
34. Big Mac topping
35. Ballerina's hairstyle
36. Alphabetic trio
37. Sailor's top
42. Big name in plastic?
43. Unaccomplished
45. Affectedly aesthetic
46. "Don't reckon so"
47. "Puss in Boots" villain
48. "The Untouchables" crime fighter Eliot
49. "The Longest Day" extras
50. Acronym on a shuttle

DOWN

1. Be a swindler
2. 11-mem. oil cartel
3. Bollywood tune
4. Gossipy gathering
5. Art supply
6. Broad avenue, briefly
7. Apparent
8. Form a line
9. A Swiss army knife has many
10. Aimless
11. Be profitable
16. It's on the tip of your tongue
19. Conventional
22. "Jeopardy!" rarity
23. "M*A*S*H" staff
24. Absorbed, as a cost
25. "You've Got Mail" company
26. French affirmative
27. "Support Our Heroes" group
28. "Down for the count" count
30. Saying it's not so
31. Having an advantage
35. Cake-and-ice-cream occasions, for short

36. Miss Marple finds them

37. Bog down

38. Believers of some stripe

39. ___ B'rith

40. Big name in arcade games

41. Screws up

42. Abigail ___ Buren

44. 4:00 English drink

Answers on page 191.

MARKET LEADERS

ACROSS

1. Clown
5. Gypsum painting surface
10. It turns litmus red
14. Avalon, according to myth
15. Clinging type
16. All's alternative
17. Flea eliminator
19. Its symbol is an inverted triangle
20. Excessively affected
21. First class?
23. Centenary of George V's coronation
25. Oater watering holes
26. Walked confidently
31. Croquet surface
32. Airborne toys
33. The sea, to Poseidon
35. Shipping letters
38. It's pumped at the gym
39. Way past the "use by" date
40. Yawn inducer
41. Big Apple inits.
42. Southern anthem
43. 12-inch stick
44. "Goldfinger" fort
46. Majesty
48. Entertains at home
51. Work on hides
52. Interfered
54. Take care of
59. Jon Arbuckle's dog
60. Spider marked by a red hourglass
62. Coffee grinder
63. Water plants
64. Movie "Citizen"
65. Plantation pod
66. Hero's exploits
67. "Bette Davis _____" (Kim Carnes song)

DOWN

1. Donation
2. Norwegian capital
3. Nondairy topping
4. Heroic deed
5. Like Poe settings
6. Hydro-electric animal?
7. _____-help
8. Healing signs
9. "You don't say!"
10. No matter what:
11. Cause for coughing
12. Machu Picchu native
13. Martin and Cain
18. Deep sleeps
22. Dis
24. Canon rival
26. Outer layer
27. Bright and breezy
28. Not moving at all

29. Coop resident
30. Where some heros are made
34. Facile
36. Popular 2-colored cookie
37. Middle name in mysteries
39. Motley assortment
40. Sloppy joe holder
42. Camay alternative
43. Get more out of Life?
45. _____ motel (place for an affair)

47. Potato dishes
48. Device tested on Bikini Atoll in 1954
49. Broadcast's sound portion
50. Moon valley
53. Haggard horses
55. "Swoosh" company
56. Invasion time
57. Use of pitch in speaking
58. Is in hock
61. Jaguar or ocelot

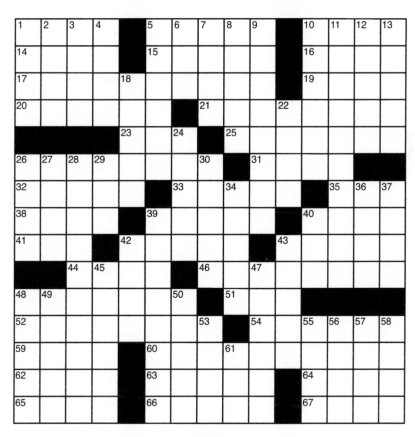

Answers on page 191.

VIVID PHRASES

ACROSS

1. Fries or coleslaw, typically
8. "Amen, brother!"
9. Classic German camera
10. Squelches early
12. "Nothing runs like a ___" (ad slogan)
14. Company dishes
16. Sealed shut
19. Bavarian souvenir
20. ___ dinner (it's supplied by guests)
21. Nicholson's breakout movie

DOWN

1. Moonlight melody
2. Find, as artifacts
3. Long-shot possibility
4. Give to a fund
5. Carnival thriller
6. Reaction producers
7. "Moby Dick" whaler
11. Knockout punch
13. Plain to see
15. Argentine plains
17. Type of song or trip
18. Aruba or Jamaica

Answers on page 192.

HOW MUCH IS THERE?

ACROSS

1. Widespread panic
9. Hotel area
10. Barely used
11. Foreman's assistant
12. Room renter
13. With 20-Across, what you're good at
15. Figure enhancer
19. Bit of chill
20. See 13-Across
22. Kind of rap
23. Finals, for example
24. Decibel control

DOWN

2. Shady spot
3. Skeptic's comeback
4. Alert color
5. Movie shots
6. Get out of hand
7. City on the Nile
8. Yukon neighbor
14. You'd hear it in Toledo
16. Haifa inhabitant
17. "Despite all that . . ."
18. Bits of broccoli
19. Mideast desert region
20. English racing town
21. Hayes of "South Park"

Answers on page 192.

FAST FOOD, HASTY READING

ACROSS

1. With 9-Across, coin stamper?
5. Disney deer
8. Rack up
9. See 1-Across
10. With 18-Across, little white lie?
11. Maiden name preceder
13. Suffix with deposit or reposit
14. Having a tin ear
16. Dance under a bar
18. See 10-Across
21. With 24-Across, cowardly caretakers?
22. Defeated one's cry
23. Bloodhound's guide
24. See 21-Across

DOWN

1. Cotton on a stick
2. Place for a keystone
3. Trunk of Charles Atlas photos
4. Eagerly unwrap
5. More gloomy
6. Pietà figure
7. Where shekels are spent
12. Be successful in life
14. Car trunk item
15. Ladies' man
17. Pilgrim's corn
18. Sister of La Toya
19. When prompted
20. It's sometimes more

Answers on page 192.

ODE TO A GRECIAN -ERN

ACROSS

1. With 8-Across, a seabird abstaining?
7. Earth's lowest point
8. See 1-Across
9. With 11-Across, Swiss town of tough interrogation?
10. Got less intense
11. See 9-Across
15. Seeks in a dictionary, e.g.
18. Web-based business
21. Site for three men in a tub
22. With 23-Across, identification of trumpeter Laura?
23. See 22-Across
24. Secret romantic encounters

DOWN

1. Like "Romeo and Juliet"
2. Ash, for example
3. Out of control
4. Some apples
5. Changer of locks?
6. Gun or bayonet
7. Moral obligation
12. Glasses and such
13. Ready to go
14. V-8 ingredient
16. Drop in for a sec
17. Put in a good word for
19. Revival shouts
20. Golf course

Answers on page 192.

ANSWERS

Comfy at Home (pages 4–5)

W	A	R	D		P	O	P		H	A	F	T
A	C	A	I		I	P	A		I	R	I	S
A	T	M	S		X	E	R		G	I	N	A
C	A	P	T	A	I	N	S	C	H	A	I	R
			U	K	E		L	A	C			
W	H	E	R	E		L	E	S		C	D	S
P	O	T	B	E	L	L	Y	S	T	O	V	E
M	I	C		L	I	D		I	O	N	I	A
		J	A	B		E	N	O				
F	E	A	T	H	E	R	P	I	L	L	O	W
R	E	F	I		R	E	C		B	A	S	H
E	L	A	L		A	N	O		O	I	S	E
E	Y	R	E		L	O	T		X	R	A	Y

Magical World of Tea (pages 6–7)

A	G	I	S	T		C	H	E	W	O	F	F
L	U	N	A		E	L	E	V		A	E	R
A	N	K	H		G	R	E	E	N	T	E	A
S	P	Y	I	N	G		D	N	A			
	O		B	A	I	O		T	I	D	A	L
K	W	A		S	E	A	M		L	I	F	E
E	D	S		A	S	S	A	M		L	T	V
R	E	E	K		T	I	R	E		L	E	O
F	R	A	U	D		S	L	A	M		R	
			D	O	S		E	T	E	R	N	E
I	N	F	U	S	I	O	N		R	O	O	T
P	I	O		E	N	C	E		C	M	O	N
S	M	O	L	D	E	R		H	Y	E	N	A

In the Kitchen (pages 8–9)

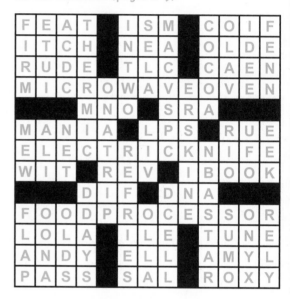

F	E	A	T		I	S	M		C	O	I	F
I	T	C	H		N	E	A		O	L	D	E
R	U	D	E		T	L	C		C	A	E	N
M	I	C	R	O	W	A	V	E	O	V	E	N
			M	N	O		S	R	A			
M	A	N	I	A		L	P	S		R	U	E
E	L	E	C	T	R	I	C	K	N	I	F	E
W	I	T		R	E	V		I	B	O	O	K
		D	I	F		D	N	A				
F	O	O	D	P	R	O	C	E	S	S	O	R
L	O	L	A		I	L	E		T	U	N	E
A	N	D	Y		E	L	L		A	M	Y	L
P	A	S	S		S	A	L		R	O	X	Y

Finish the Adage (pages 10–11)

C	L	U	B		A	L	E		K	N	E	W
H	A	R	E		L	I	A		L	O	R	I
A	S	S	E	N	T	E	R		I	R	I	S
W	H	A	T	Y	O	U	P	R	E	A	C	H
			L	Y	S		L	U	G			
C	O	R	E	A		J	U	S		G	A	P
G	O	O	D	N	E	I	G	H	B	O	R	S
I	O	N		K	L	M		J	E	T	T	Y
			S	E	E		O	O	H			
P	O	T	N	E	V	E	R	B	O	I	L	S
L	I	M	A		A	S	K	S	O	V	E	R
U	S	A	F		T	A	I		V	E	N	T
M	E	N	U		E	I	N		E	S	T	A

ANSWERS

American Folk Tales (pages 12–13)

S	L	A	V		A	I	D		I	S	L	A
T	A	R	O		U	N	O		S	H	I	P
A	M	A	T		G	R	U	E	S	O	M	E
B	A	B	E	T	H	E	B	L	U	E	O	X
		R	O	T		L	E	E				
R	A	D	I	O		L	E	V		D	I	M
M	A	I	D	O	F	T	H	E	M	I	S	T
N	U	N		F	E	D		N	I	K	O	N
		A	T	A		I	T	S				
J	I	G	G	E	R	J	O	H	N	S	O	N
A	L	L	I	N	F	U	N		A	L	L	Y
P	E	A	L		U	N	I		M	A	L	E
E	S	M	E		L	E	A		E	T	A	T

Pop Stars (pages 16–17)

F	I	B	S		B	I	T		S	T	L	O
O	K	L	A		A	D	O		T	R	A	P
R	E	V	I	E	W	E	R		A	U	N	T
D	A	D	D	Y	L	O	N	G	L	E	G	S
			H	E	S		A	O	K			
R	E	L	I	C		I	D	I		H	O	B
I	C	E		A	P	R	O	N		A	A	U
G	O	O		N	R	A		D	A	I	R	Y
			I	D	O		A	E	C			
D	A	D	D	Y	W	A	R	B	U	C	K	S
A	C	A	I		L	E	F	T	T	U	R	N
I	M	H	O		E	R	E		E	R	I	A
N	E	S	T		R	O	D		R	E	S	P

To Kill a Mockingbird (pages 14–15)

A	L	A	B	A	M	A		A	G	O	R	A
V	I	N	E	G	A	R		M	A	N	E	T
E	L	E	C	T	O	R		A	L	L	A	T
R	A	M	A		I	S	R	A	E	L	I	
S	C	O	U	T		B	O	O		A	T	C
	S	O	F	A	R		S	O	U			
P	E	T	E	R	I		E	S	K	E	R	S
R	U	R		N	U	R	S	E				
E	R	A		E	C	T		A	Y	E	A	R
S	A	I	D	S	H	H		P	A	W	L	
A	S	P	I	N		A	T	L	A	R	G	E
L	I	S	L	E		N	E	E	D	L	E	S
T	A	E	L	S		T	R	E	S	S	E	S

Look on the Bright Side (pages 18–19)

W	H	E	W		T	E	A		S	L	I	P
O	A	T	H		I	S	M		R	U	S	E
E	R	N	O		L	A	O		O	S	L	O
S	P	A	R	K	L	I	N	G		T	E	N
			L	E	N		G	N	A	R		
T	A	D		N	O	T		U	S	O	F	A
S	H	A	M		W	W	W		S	U	I	T
K	A	Z	O	O		O	A	K		S	E	E
		Z	E	R	O		L	I	V			
P	O	L		B	R	I	L	L	I	A	N	T
E	M	I	L		A	P	E		V	O	U	S
K	A	N	E		T	O	Y		I	N	K	A
E	R	G	O		E	S	E		D	E	E	R

ANSWERS

It's in Your Hands (pages 20–21)

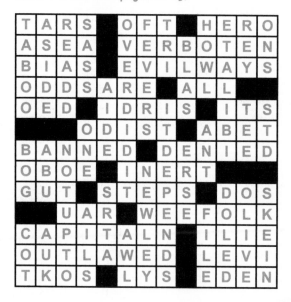

```
F O O D   C H O C   T A P
I D L E   L E A H   E T E
T I L L   A P S O   E R N
A N A L Y S T   P A N I C
S G S   O P A   S C I F I
    H U E D   T C E L L
P I C A R D   M I T R E S
A H A L F   H I C S
P A R E U   A L K   G D S
E V E N T   M E S S I A H
E E E   U S M A   U T N E
T I R   R O E G   E M I L
E T S   E I R E   T O O L
```

Baddies of Fiction (pages 24–25)

```
L A V A   F E N   E M I T
E V I L   L E E   P E P A
D I E T   Y E W   S N O B
  S W E E N E Y T O D D
        R A N   E I N
M I N E R   R A J   K E G
F R E D D Y K R U E G E R
A R T   R O O   A M B L E
    H U G   O N O
  N O R M A N B A T E S
B O N O   M E A   I M O K
S I C S   A R M   O M N I
A R E S   T O A   N A S A
```

That's a No-No (pages 22–23)

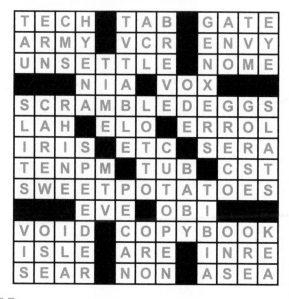

```
T A R S   O F T   H E R O
A S E A   V E R B O T E N
B I A S   E V I L W A Y S
O D D S A R E   A L L
O E D   I D R I S   I T S
    O D I S T   A B E T
B A N N E D   D E N I E D
O B O E   I N E R T
G U T   S T E P S   D O S
    U A R   W E E F O L K
C A P I T A L N   I L I E
O U T L A W E D   L E V I
T K O S   L Y S   E D E N
```

What's Cooking (pages 26–27)

```
T E C H   T A B   G A T E
A R M Y   V C R   E N V Y
U N S E T T L E   N O M E
    N I A   V O X
S C R A M B L E D E G G S
L A H   E L O   E R R O L
I R I S   E T C   S E R A
T E N P M   T U B   C S T
S W E E T P O T A T O E S
    E V E   O B I
V O I D   C O P Y B O O K
I S L E   A R E   I N R E
S E A R   N O N   A S E A
```

ANSWERS

Strictly PC (pages 28–29)

M	O	T	E	■	A	M	I	■	Q	U	I	Z
C	O	A	X	■	N	I	L	■	U	N	T	O
S	O	U	P	N	A	Z	I	■	I	C	E	E
■	■	O	U	R	■	A	T	E	■	■	■	■
P	R	A	W	N	C	O	C	K	T	A	I	L
R	A	T	■	N	H	L	■	O	U	N	C	E
E	D	A	M	■	Y	E	T	■	S	N	A	G
O	A	R	E	D	■	I	V	Y	■	A	R	G
P	R	I	N	C	E	C	H	A	R	L	E	S
■	O	V	A	■	O	L	E	■	■	■	■	■
Y	A	W	N	■	R	O	S	E	M	A	R	Y
E	V	I	L	■	T	U	T	■	I	S	L	E
H	A	Z	Y	■	H	I	S	■	T	A	S	S

Hit Songs (pages 32–33)

T	E	L	L	■	S	R	S	■	I	D	L	E
O	T	O	E	■	I	O	N	■	G	E	O	S
R	A	M	I	■	R	B	I	■	L	A	P	P
A	T	A	S	T	E	O	F	H	O	N	E	Y
■	■	U	R	N	■	T	O	O	■	■	■	■
P	E	T	R	I	■	E	E	L	■	G	A	P
B	L	U	E	B	E	R	R	Y	H	I	L	L
S	K	G	■	O	A	R	■	M	A	N	L	Y
■	■	A	R	T	■	B	A	G	■	■	■	■
I	T	S	N	O	W	O	R	N	E	V	E	R
B	R	I	G	■	E	R	A	■	R	I	M	E
I	O	N	E	■	L	E	G	■	T	V	M	A
S	U	E	R	■	L	O	G	■	Y	E	A	R

Horse Operas (pages 30–31)

A	D	E	N	■	P	I	E	■	P	L	A	N
T	I	P	I	■	A	D	M	■	L	A	C	Y
A	S	E	A	■	W	E	E	■	I	N	R	E
T	H	E	L	O	N	E	R	A	N	G	E	R
■	■	O	W	S	■	I	L	K	■	■	■	■
G	W	Y	N	N	■	A	T	L	■	I	C	U
T	H	E	G	U	N	F	I	G	H	T	E	R
O	O	P	■	P	E	T	■	O	A	T	E	N
■	■	I	T	O	■	C	N	N	■	■	■	■
F	A	S	T	O	N	T	H	E	D	R	A	W
A	B	I	G	■	O	I	L	■	B	U	O	Y
H	U	T	U	■	I	D	O	■	A	N	N	S
D	D	A	Y	■	R	Y	E	■	G	E	E	S

Characters We Love (pages 34–35)

S	P	E	C	■	O	W	L	S	■	H	I	D
T	A	C	O	■	U	H	O	H	■	E	D	U
U	P	O	N	■	T	I	V	O	■	R	E	T
N	A	N	C	Y	D	R	E	W	■	M	A	Y
■	■	L	O	O	■	D	E	M	I	■	■	■
C	A	J	U	N	■	T	I	R	E	O	U	T
B	R	A	D	■	S	I	T	■	A	N	T	S
S	E	N	E	G	A	L	■	S	N	E	A	K
■	■	E	D	A	M	■	D	O	W	■	■	■
O	B	E	■	R	O	B	I	N	H	O	O	D
P	A	Y	■	A	V	E	R	■	I	D	L	E
E	R	R	■	G	A	N	G	■	L	O	I	N
N	E	E	■	E	R	T	E	■	E	R	O	S

ANSWERS

Holding Hands (pages 36–37)

C	O	M	P		W	E	T		H	U	G	E
O	P	A	L		I	R	S		A	X	I	S
Y	E	T	I		L	I	E		R	O	T	E
	C	H	A	N	D	E	L	I	E	R	S	
		B	E	E		I	S	M				
P	O	U	L	T		K	O	S		M	A	Y
T	A	M	E		L	I	T		C	O	R	E
A	R	P		R	E	X		W	H	I	C	H
		F	A	B		A	W	E				
	W	A	S	H	A	N	D	W	E	A	R	
T	I	N	T		R	E	D		S	L	A	P
A	L	T	O		O	R	E		E	E	R	O
P	E	E	P		N	O	D		S	E	E	P

Fun Fads (pages 40–41)

I	T	S		C	O	B	S		A	D	E	S
H	U	L	A	H	O	O	P		L	E	V	I
O	N	A	S	L	O	P	E		E	B	A	N
P	A	T	I	O		P	E	T	R	O	C	K
		A	E	C		D	I	O	N			
H	O	G	G		A	I	D	S		A	I	L
T	A	R	O		M	O	I		J	I	B	E
S	K	A		A	P	I	A		A	R	M	S
		V	E	R	B		L	A	W			
C	H	I	A	P	E	T		T	O	G	A	S
N	O	T	V		L	O	O	P	H	O	L	E
B	R	A	E		L	A	V	A	L	A	M	P
C	A	S	S		S	T	A	R		L	S	T

Guess the Theme (pagse 38—39)

B	E	E	P		S	O	N		T	Y	R	O
U	T	E	S		C	P	U		H	O	O	P
M	A	R	Y		O	A	R		R	Y	A	S
	L	O	C	K	T	H	E	D	O	O	R	
		H	O	T		Y	E	W				
P	A	T	I	O		G	E	L		H	E	R
S	T	O	C	K	D	I	V	I	D	E	N	D
I	M	P		I	O	N		V	O	T	E	S
		E	E	L		T	E	N				
	B	A	R	R	E	L	O	R	G	A	N	
P	U	M	A		O	A	K		L	O	O	T
E	R	O	S		U	S	A		E	N	D	S
T	Y	K	E		T	H	Y		S	E	E	P

Fictional Places (pages 42—43)

U	S	B		S	E	G	A		F	L	A	T
S	E	A		P	I	L	L		R	O	L	O
C	A	B	E	R	N	E	T		O	T	T	O
G	U	A	V	A		E	A	R	T	H	E	N
		E	N	G		C	H	A	R	T		
S	H	A	N	G	R	I	L	A		R	E	O
T	A	U	T		R	O	E		B	I	G	W
E	M	T		B	R	I	G	A	D	O	O	N
P	R	O	S	Y		O	S	U				
F	A	R	O	U	K	I		H	B	O	M	B
O	D	A	Y		I	M	P	O	S	T	O	R
R	I	C	A		S	O	A	R		I	O	N
D	O	E	S		S	K	Y	E		S	N	O

ANSWERS

Rhyme Time (pages 44–45)

```
D E S K █ A S H █ U S E S
U C L A █ L O O █ T E R I
B R O W N C O W █ O M I T
S U G A R A N D S P I C E
█ █ I A N █ E L I A █ █
A L F █ █ E D U A R D O
N A U G H T Y O R N I C E
O V E R A W E █ █ D V D
█ █ L I L O █ S R I █ █
R O L L O F T H E D I C E
E V I L █ E P I C T A L E
P I N E █ E E N █ A G O G
O D E R █ T D S █ G O D S
```

Advertising Mascots (pages 48–49)

```
N E T █ F A R █ G L A S S
E D A M A M E █ O A T E S
R E T I R E D █ O S A G E
F R I T O B A N D I T O █
█ █ T E A N E C K █ █
D Y N E █ S T A R █ D A D
J O H N F █ █ Y O U R S
S N L █ U S S R █ N O E L
█ █ G L U C O S E █ █
█ C H E F B O Y A R D E E
O M A N I █ F A T U I T Y
A V R I L █ F L A N K E R
F I D E L █ S S N █ E S E
```

Driving Around (pages 46–47)

```
S A S S I N G █ L E A P T
I D I D T O O █ U L T R A
D I C I E S T █ X Y L E M
E E E █ T A B U █ A T T
B U M P E R C A R █ N E A
█ U S A █ S Y S T E M
F L I R T █ C Y A N S
L I N E A L █ P A N █
A V A █ T E N O R C L E F
T E T █ E D I T █ A R E
B O R I C █ P A R T I A L
E N O L A █ A G A I N S T
D E T E R █ T E E P E E S
```

13-letter Words (pages 50–51)

```
P E T █ L A M B █ P O O L
A P R █ E S A I █ A N N A
R I O █ M O S T █ D E E S
A C U P U N C T U R I S T
█ E R E █ E V E N L Y
C U R E S █ B R A █ T I E
A N O N █ A Y N █ D E C A
R E B █ G R E █ S A N E R
P R O T E M █ U P N █
O R N I T H O L O G I S T
R I A L █ O D O R █ W I I
T N U T █ L I C K █ I T D
S G T S █ E E K S █ N E E
```

ANSWERS

Ho! (pages 52–53)

```
I O W A   O L D   L A S H
T T O P   V I I   A R I A
C R O P L A N D   W E A N
H O L L Y   E N G L A N D
      Y O U   T O E
D A Y   N A B   O S I E R
E D A M   R I D   S O M E
C O P R A   N O D   N U T
      C D S   N E T
G A R L A N D   S I C K O
E R I E   A U C K L A N D
E T T A   C P O   E G A D
K E E N   K E G   X E R S
```

Pull (pages 56–57)

```
S A N D R A B U L L O C K
  M   O   U   N   I   O
C O V E R S   I N F A N T
  U   T   T   E   M
O N E H O R S E   S E A M
  T   I   I   T   N
      G R A V I T Y
  P   H   N   L   S
Z I N C   P R I C E W A R
  R   H   T   A   T
B A Z A A R   I G E T I T
  T   I   S   C   R
G E O R G E C L O O N E Y
```

Family Entertainment (pages 54–55)

```
  R E B A M C E N T I R E
A   R   S E A   N   A
T O R C H   L O S E S I T
  T   O   A   E   U
A I R T R A V E L   C U P
C   A   I   T
K E L L Y C L A R K S O N
    I   L   I   O
K O P   G O A L P O S T S
A   S   I   S   E   H
B A Y O N E T   O U T D O
O   N   S   I   F   W
B E C A U S E O F Y O U
```

The Breakfast Club (pages 58–59)

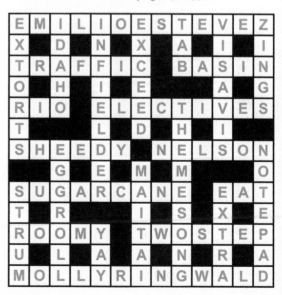

```
E M I L I O E S T E V E Z
X   D   N   X   A   I   I
T R A F F I C   B A S I N
O   H   I   E       A   G
R I O   E L E C T I V E S
T       L   D   H   I
S H E E D Y   N E L S O N
    G   E   M   M       O
S U G A R C A N E   E A T
T   R   I   S   X   E
R O O M Y   T W O S T E P
U   L   A   A   N   R   A
M O L L Y R I N G W A L D
```

ANSWERS

It's All in How You Read It (pages 60–61)

L	E	A	H		D	O	A		G	O	B	S
A	R	L	O		U	R	N		E	L	A	H
W	I	I	G		M	E	A		N	E	N	E
N	E	I	G	H	B	O	R	H	O	O	D	
	I	B	O			C	I	A				
T	O	R	S	O		V	H	S		F	A	T
U	H	O	H		D	I	Y		B	O	S	H
T	M	I		P	E	A		A	R	O	S	E
		A	I	M		E	R	A				
	S	U	B	C	O	N	S	C	I	O	U	S
F	A	S	O		T	O	T		D	E	R	M
A	G	E	D		E	T	E		E	N	D	O
B	A	S	E		D	E	E		D	O	U	G

Getting Arty (pages 64–65)

S	L	A	P		V	M	I		N	O	T	E
L	A	Z	E		E	A	R		A	D	A	M
A	D	I	N		T	H	A	W	S	O	U	T
B	Y	Z	A	N	T	I	N	E	A	R	T	
		N	E	E		I	L	L				
A	M	O	C	O		P	A	L		A	A	U
C	A	V	E	P	A	I	N	T	I	N	G	S
E	R	A		H	I	T		O	N	I	O	N
		O	Y	L		O	D	D				
	C	O	N	T	E	M	P	O	R	A	R	Y
F	O	R	T	E	R	I	E		I	R	I	S
L	I	Z	A		O	A	R		V	I	S	E
A	T	O	P		N	S	A		E	D	E	R

Gone Fishin' (pages 62–63)

S	A	L	M	O	N		W	H	A	L	E	S
T	R	Y	O	N	E		B	Y	R	O	T	E
O	T	E	L	L	O		C	A	T	B	O	X
W	E	S	T	E	N	D		T	D	S		
		S	A	A	B		T	E	T	R	A	
E	E	L		S	T	A	R		C	E	O	S
A	Z	A	L	E	A		A	C	O	R	N	S
T	I	R	E		L	A	V	A		S	A	T
S	O	G	G	Y		S	I	R	S			
	E	A	U		P	O	W	E	R	P	C	
C	A	S	T	R	O		L	A	G	U	N	A
O	N	S	E	T	S		I	S	A	D	O	R
D	O	E	S	S	O		S	H	R	I	M	P

Finish the Adage (2) (pages 66–67)

J	O	N	I		E	W	E		D	R	O	Z
E	C	O	N		X	I	N		R	U	L	A
H	A	R	D	C	A	S	H		I	B	I	S
U	S	W	E	L	L	C	A	L	L	Y	O	U
			P	E	T		N	I	L			
L	C	D	T	V		A	C	V		D	E	W
I	S	T	H	E	S	W	E	E	T	E	S	T
T	I	S		R	U	E		N	I	X	E	S
		P	E	R		T	S	P				
B	E	F	O	R	E	Y	O	U	L	E	A	P
O	L	E	O		B	U	M	P	I	N	T	O
D	I	S	C		E	L	S		N	O	O	N
S	E	T	H		T	E	K		E	S	M	E

ANSWERS

The Next Big Thing (pages 68–69)

```
M A S S I V E █ H A S T A
I M P E R I L █ U B O A T
S A L I E R I █ M C D L T
E T A S █ T O D O █ A L A
R I T █ G U T E N █ L I I
█ █ D I E █ N G U Y E N █
A S P E N █ █ O P E D S
B A L B O A █ D U C █ █ █
O V A █ R A M U S █ S S E
L A N █ M A A M █ M O O R
I N T R O █ O D W A L L A
S N A F U █ R U I N O U S
H A R K S █ I M M E N S E
```

Find the City (pages 72–73)

```
C L I M A T E █ L E G G S
P I T A P A T █ U T R A P
L A S T O R Y █ S T A L E
U N I T █ █ M U T A B L E
S E T O N █ O H S █ F E D
█ █ █ C I G N A █ O O O
T I C K L E █ U T U R N S
O N O █ █ T A L K S █ █ █
O C T █ T I N █ O S C A R
S L E W I N G █ █ C A V E
L U R I E █ L A V O R I S
O D I N G █ E N C L O S E
W E E D S █ D A R E N O T
```

12-string Guitar (pages 70–71)

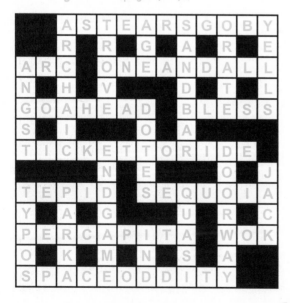

```
█ A S T E A R S G O B Y
█ R █ R █ G █ A █ R █ E
A R C █ O N E A N D A L L
N █ H █ V █ D █ T █ L
G O A H E A D █ B L E S S
S █ I █ O █ A
T I C K E T T O R I D E
█ N █ E █ █ O █ J
T E P I D █ S E Q U O I A
Y █ A █ G █ U █ R █ C
P E R C A P I T A █ W O K
O █ K █ M █ N █ S █ A
S P A C E O D D I T Y
```

Sir Richard (pages 74–75)

```
J U R A S S I C P A R K █
A █ A █ T █ Q █ I █ E █ I
M O P █ E A S T E R E G G
A █ I █ W █ █ C █ L █ E
I N D I A █ S E E T O I T
C █ R █ T █ █ █ F
A B R I D G E T O O F A R
█ E █ █ W █ N █ U
B A D N E W S █ A W A R D
A █ C █ R █ T █ D █ O
B L O W A F U S E █ I L L
Y █ A █ S █ R █ A █ P
█ A T T E N B O R O U G H
```

ANSWERS

A Pair of Movies (pages 76–77)

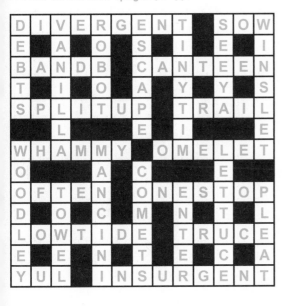

Hidden Clue (pages 80–81)

Even as We Spock (pages 78–79)

Good-bye, Good Buy (pages 82–83)

ANSWERS

The Americans (pages 84–85)

Rock and Roll Hall of Fame (pages 88–89)

Misnomers (pages 86–87)

Two Men and a Lovely Lady (pages 90–91)

ANSWERS

Hodgepodge (pages 92–93)

	F	A	L	L	E	N	A	N	G	E	L	
	I		E		A		W	O	E		E	
G	N	A	T		S	E	A	R	C	H	M	E
	E		B		Y		Y		A		O	
	T	H	E	L	M	A		W	R	E	N	
	O			A		L		T		A		
H	O	T	A	I	R		O	N	S	I	D	E
	T		R		K		O			E		
H	A	C	K		S	K	A	T	E	S		
C		H		A		U		O		T		
P	O	L	A	R	C	A	P		G	D	A	Y
	M		I		M		T		U		N	
B	A	C	H	E	L	O	R	P	A	D		

X Marks the Spot (pages 94–95)

L	E	T	G	O	O	F		F	S	T	O	P
A		R		N		I		A		E		E
Y	O	Y	O	S		E	N	D	U	S	E	R
E			I		T		L		E		T	K
G	A	T	O	R	A	D	E		F	R	A	Y
G			I		E		P		U			
S	T	O	C	K	E	X	C	H	A	N	G	E
		I		E		E		O				A
T	A	L	K		B	R	I	N	G	O	U	T
B		D		W		C		E		F		D
A	I	R	T	A	X	I		T	U	T	T	I
L		U		R		S		A		W		R
L	E	M	O	N		E	D	G	E	O	U	T

Common Phrases (pages 96–97)

D	I	R	T	F	A	R	M		B	A	S	S
A		U		O		U			L		L	
T	A	B	O	O		B	A	D	M	O	V	E
E		Y		T		L		O		H		E
			R	U	B	B	E	R	S	T	A	M	P
H		E		A		S		A				O
A	N	D	A	L	L		E	N	G	U	L	F
N				L		L		D		L		F
D	A	Y	A	F	T	E	R	D	A	Y		
E		E		A		A		O		S		D
D	R	A	W	N	O	N		N	O	S	I	R
I		R			T		T		E			A
N	O	S	Y		H	O	U	S	E	S	I	T

Jobs and Industries (pages 98–99)

S	T	E	W	A	R	T		A	L	P	H	A
H		N		U		A		A		H		S
I	N	V	E	S	T	I	G	A	T	O	R	S
N		I		T		W			T			I
E	A	R		R	E	A	C	T	I	O	N	S
		O		A		N		O		G		T
D	O	N	A	L	D		A	L	E	R	T	S
E		M		I		E		E		A		
A	L	E	X	A	N	D	E	R		P	O	P
L		N			W		A			H		A
E	N	T	E	R	T	A	I	N	M	E	N	T
R		A		A		R		C		R		H
S	A	L	E	M		D	R	E	S	S	E	S

ANSWERS

A Glitzy Lifestyle (pages 100–101)

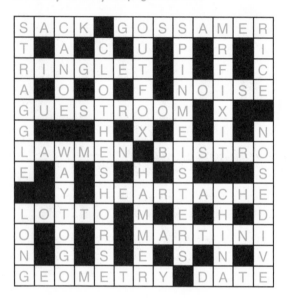

Evocative Phrases (pages 104–105)

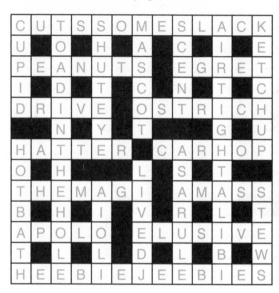

Stories and Sayings (pages 102–103)

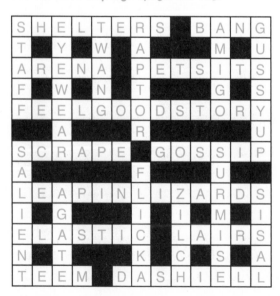

Some of the Best Pictures (pages 106–107)

Rhyme Time 2 (pages 108–109)

```
E T T A   L E S T   T R I
A R A B   E L K O   R E V
S E E S   O L Y M P I C S
T A B O O   A R E A S
  T O R A H   O I L E R S
  B R O N C   E C C E
F O O   S T O K E   T A T
D U N S   P R E S S
R I A L T O   T A I N T
  L U N C H   I N U I T
C H E R O K E E   B R E R
E A R   T E A S   A S I A
O R T   E T R E   D E N Y
```

Oxymorons (pages 112–113)

```
F   T   H A T F I E L D S
L   V   A     D   E   A
A L M A N A C   L E G O S
P   O   G     E   U   S
J U M B O   S H R I M P
A   U         E   L
C R A F T Y   I T A S C A
K   N         R     B
R A N D O M   O R D E R
S   G   I     U   O   A
T O R T S   B U N G L E D
U   A   C     C   L   O
B A M B O O Z L E   S   R
```

He Wrote the Songs (pages 110–111)

```
B A R R Y M A N I L O W
O   A   A   L   V   N   B
M U Z A K   I C E D T E A
B   O   E   B     H   G
S U R E T H I N G   E Y E
    Y   S   O     G   L
M A N D Y     L O O K S
A   A   A   D   D
S K I   K N I F E E D G E
H   R     M   N   R   J
E G O T R I P   E X I L E
D   B   Y   L   R   V   C
  L I K E W E M A D E I T
```

Characters and Phrases (pages 114–115)

```
M A A N D P A K E T T L E
A   S   E   P     S   X
R A T R A C E   S H E E P
I   R   D   M     L   O
A B O D E   A C A C I A S
          Y   N   O   E
C R A N E S   C A C T U S
L   G     P   B
A W E S O M E   O P A L S
S   S   S   E   L   N   A
S A A B S   W A I K I K I
I   G     E   S   S   L
C O O L O N E S H E E L S
```

Leading Men (pages 116–117)

```
A S C O T S █ L G S
R I P R A P █ I R E
P A U L N E W M A N
A M S O █ C A P T S
█ █ █ G I L L I E
E R R O L F L Y N N
T E A P O Y █ █ █ █
C R I E R █ M E I R
H E N R Y F O N D A
E N O █ B A R E L Y
S T N █ E N T R E E
```

How to Take Charge (pages 120–121)

```
W A N D A █ I C I C L E
A C E I T █ C A L L O N
R U L E T H E R O O S T
M E S S H A L L █ T E E
█ █ █ █ E A T █ W H I R
C A L L T H E S H O T S
O D A S █ █ L O O █
N O L █ D E A R S I R S
C R A C K T H E W H I P
H E L E N A █ S H I V A
S E A L Y S █ T O T E M
```

Broadway Musicals (pages 118–119)

```
S O P H █ B E L A
O L L A █ O D O N
H A A S █ O N E O
O N T H E T O W N
█ █ T A H R █
A I M A T █ T W A
B R I G A D O O N
C A L █ W O N K A
█ D I A G █
F U N N Y G I R L
A R E S █ O R E O
V I S E █ N O N U
A S S T █ E N I D
```

Common Phrases (pages 122–123)

```
C O R N C O B █ L U C I D
H █ O █ O █ U █ H █ E
A F T E R A F A S H I O N
S █ U █ R █ F █ V █ S
S E N T I N E L █ F E T E
I █ D █ D █ T █ A █ █
S H A L O M █ A S I M O V
█ █ R █ T █ I █ O █
B R A T █ B U T T O N I T
O █ L █ T █ W █ G █ E
W O L F A T T H E D O O R
L █ A █ U R █ L █
S A Y H I █ T R E A S O N
```

Tom Hanks Movies (pages 124–125)

```
P O S T ■ B E N ■ S T L O
N I L E ■ L I E ■ C A A N
O L I P H A N T ■ A I D S
M Y D E A R ■ S U L L Y ■
■ ■ E W E ■ U S E S ■
B E D ■ ■ G R O U P O N
B R I D G E O F S P I E S
C A S E L A W ■ ■ ■ N R A
■ C H A T ■ A D V ■
■ C L O U D ■ B A I L E Y
F E A R ■ I N C H O A T E
A D I N ■ R I T ■ L I O N
D E M S ■ T A V ■ A N N S
```

Back-to-Back Victories (pages 128–129)

Good Shows (pages 126–127)

```
T A M P A ■ L A P S E
E L I H U ■ A P R E S
M A R Y P O P P I N S
P R E L A W ■ L O D E
■ L I N A ■ R I N
A C H O R U S L I N E
G A O ■ S P C A ■
A S T O ■ T E C H I E
T H E L I O N K I N G
H E L E N ■ T E S S A
A S S O C ■ S Y N O D
```

Double Vision (pages 130–131)

ANSWERS

Parasite (pages 132–133)

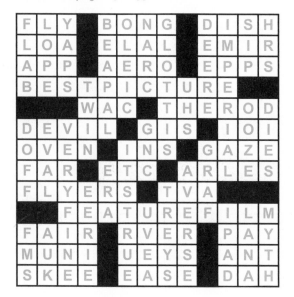

F	L	Y		B	O	N	G		D	I	S	H
L	O	A		E	L	A	L		E	M	I	R
A	P	P		A	E	R	O		E	P	P	S
B	E	S	T	P	I	C	T	U	R	E		
			W	A	C		T	H	E	R	O	D
D	E	V	I	L		G	I	S		I	O	I
O	V	E	N		I	N	S		G	A	Z	E
F	A	R		E	T	C		A	R	L	E	S
F	L	Y	E	R	S		T	V	A			
		F	E	A	T	U	R	E	F	I	L	M
F	A	I	R		R	V	E	R		P	A	Y
M	U	N	I		U	E	Y	S		A	N	T
S	K	E	E		E	A	S	E		D	A	H

In a Rush (pages 136–137)

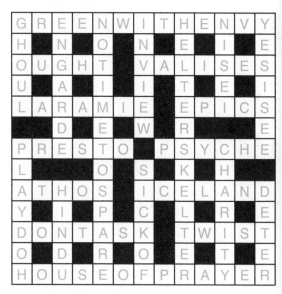

G	R	E	E	N	W	I	T	H	E	N	V	Y
H		N		O		N		E		I		E
O	U	G	H	T		V	A	L	I	S	E	S
U		A		I		I		T		E		I
L	A	R	A	M	I	E		E	P	I	C	S
		D		E		W		R				E
P	R	E	S	T	O		P	S	Y	C	H	E
L			O		S		K		H			
A	T	H	O	S		I	C	E	L	A	N	D
Y		I		P		C		L		R		E
D	O	N	T	A	S	K		T	W	I	S	T
O			D		R		O		E		T	E
H	O	U	S	E	O	F	P	R	A	Y	E	R

Middle-Name Stars (pages 134–135)

M	O	A	T		B	A	R	B	S
A	S	T	A		I	S	I	A	H
C	L	A	R	K	G	A	B	L	E
S	O	T	T	O		P	E	L	E
			A	R	T		R	E	N
R	O	O	N	E	Y	M	A	R	A
H	C	L		A	S	A			
O	T	I	S		O	N	I	C	E
D	A	V	I	D	N	I	V	E	N
E	V	I	A	N		L	A	N	G
S	E	A	M	Y		A	N	T	S

Three 45s (pages 138–139)

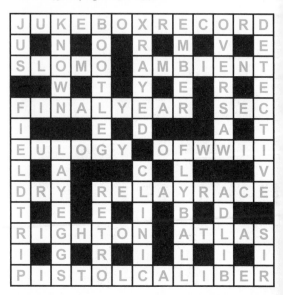

J	U	K	E	B	O	X	R	E	C	O	R	D
U		N		O		R		M		V		E
S	L	O	M	O		A	M	B	I	E	N	T
		W		T		Y		E		R		E
F	I	N	A	L	Y	E	A	R		S	E	C
I			E		D		D		A			T
E	U	L	O	G	Y		O	F	W	W	I	I
L		A			C		L		V
D	R	Y		R	E	L	A	Y	R	A	C	E
T		E		E		I		B		D	
R	I	G	H	T	O	N		A	T	L	A	S
I		G		R		I		L		I	
P	I	S	T	O	L	C	A	L	I	B	E	R

188

Apple Core (pages 140–141)

	L	I	P	S	M	A	C	K	I	N	G
	O		A		R		E		C		R
B	A	N	A	N	A	S		N	E	A	T	O
A		G		I			T		N		U
N	B	A		C	L	I	M	A	C	T	I	C
K		R		R		U				C		H
	M	A	R	D	I	G	R	A	S			
U			E		S			U		S	
S	T	O	M	A	C	H	E	D		N	A	M
E		R		L			R		D		O
S	U	S	H	I		M	O	O	R	I	N	G
U		O		S		A		W		A	
P	A	N	A	M	A	C	A	N	A	L	

Apt Anagrams (pages 144–145)

A	R	N	O		S	H	A	G
C	H	E	R		L	E	I	A
D	E	B	I	T	C	A	R	D
C	O	R	G	I		D	I	F
			A	M	S	T	E	L
D	O	R	M	I	T	O	R	Y
O	N	E	I	D	A			
N	H	A		E	T	H	A	N
T	O	M	C	R	U	I	S	E
G	L	E	N		E	R	I	E
O	D	D	S		S	E	N	D

Grandma's Pantry (pages 142–143)

S	H	I	M		I	S	S		M	A	M	A
P	E	T	A		S	K	A		E	D	A	M
O	X	E	N		H	U	D		D	U	N	E
O		M	A	R	M	A	L	A	D	E		N
N		G	O	A		Y	U	L		C	
F	A	C	E	T	E	D		K	E	Y	U	P
U	S	B		L	U	M			E	R	R
L	O	C	U	M		B	A	G	A	S	S	E
	F		B	I	O		R	N	D		S
I		C	O	N	F	I	T	U	R	E		E
S	T	O	A		F	B	I		I	N	C	R
B	A	L	T		A	I	A		A	Z	O	V
N	U	T	S		L	D	L		N	O	T	E

Hello, Aussies (pages 146–147)

T	A	K	E		E	M	S	P	A	C	E
I	D	O	L		P	L	A	T	Y	P	U	S
B	L	A	U		O	R	N	A	M	E	N	T
B	I	L	L	A	B	O	N	G		M	E	R
S	B	A		O	O	P	S		A	A	A
		C	R	Y	O		T	E	S	T	Y
O	D	E	T	S		S	H	A	K	E	
K	U	A	L	A		W	H	I	R	
A	T	V		F	O	I	E		E	M	T
R	B	I		D	O	W	N	U	N	D	E	R
M	A	N	P	U	R	S	E		U	S	D	A
A	C	C	E	N	T	E	D		T	E	E	M
S	K	I	N	N	E	R		S	L	A	P

ANSWERS

People and Places (pages 148–149)

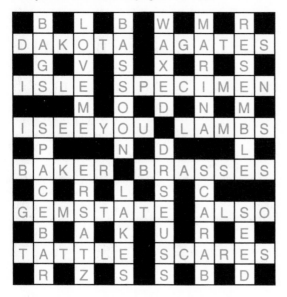

Maps and Locations (pages 152–153)

Ethan Allen's Dictionary (pages 150–151)

Frances McDormand Films (pages 154–155)

ANSWERS

Fun & Games (pages 156–157)

S	C	A	N		T	R	E	E		P	O	S	T	S
I	O	T	A		E	A	R	L		A	T	E	A	M
T	R	O	I		A	N	N	S		S	T	A	L	L
R	O	L	L	E	R	C	O	A	S	T	E	R		
E	N	L		A	S	H		P	A	R	C	E	L	
P	A	S	T	S		B	O	O		S	H	E	D	
	W	E	S		O	H	T	O		M	R	S		
	B	O	U	N	C	Y	H	O	U	S	E			
A	L	A		P	U	R	L		N	C	O			
D	E	B	I		G	T	E		H	O	R	S	E	
D	I	E	S	E	L		P	O	I		E	N	D	
	R	I	D	I	N	G	A	S	E	E	S	A	W	
W	R	U	N	G		E	L	E	C		P	A	P	A
B	E	T	T	E		R	O	S	A		I	V	O	R
C	O	H	O	S		O	W	E	R		S	E	N	D

Rhyme Time 3 (pages 160–161)

C	O	R	K		P	B	S		Q	U	I	P
O	P	A	L		A	L	E		U	S	D	A
N	E	G	A	T	I	V	E		E	E	L	Y
	C	A	T	A	N	D	M	O	U	S	E	
		S	S	T		I	R	E				
T	R	A	C	T		A	N	T		O	U	T
I	N	T	H	E	D	O	G	H	O	U	S	E
E	S	E		B	E	L		O	N	I	O	N
		B	U	N		C	D	E				
	M	I	D	D	Y	B	L	O	U	S	E	
V	I	S	A		I	N	E	X	P	E	R	T
A	R	T	Y		N	A	W		O	G	R	E
N	E	S	S		G	I	S		N	A	S	A

Mishmash (pages 158–159)

A	R	G	O	N	A	U	T		A	W	E	S
E		N		E	N		H			A		A
S	T	O	N	E	C	I	R	C	L	E		
O		M	D	Q		A		E				
P	E		L		U	P	E	N	D			
		E		E	S		L					
S	W	A	M	P	S		H	A	V	E	N	S
A		B	O		P		R					
M	A	N	I	S	E		S		C		B	
O		D		N	O		W		A		A	
A	A	F	T	E	R	D	I	N	N	E	R	
N		B		I		F	O	N				
S	W	A	G		N	A	M	E	L	E	S	S

Market Leaders (pages 162–163)

G	O	O	F		G	E	S	S	O		A	C	I	D
I	S	L	E		L	E	E	C	H		N	O	N	E
F	L	E	A	C	O	L	L	A	R		Y	M	C	A
T	O	O	T	O	O		F	R	E	S	H	M	A	N
			M	M	X		S	A	L	O	O	N	S	
S	A	S	H	A	Y	E	D		L	A	W	N		
K	I	T	E	S		R	E	A	L	M		C	O	D
I	R	O	N		M	O	L	D	Y		B	O	R	E
N	Y	C		D	I	X	I	E		R	U	L	E	R
	K	N	O	X		S	P	L	E	N	D	O	R	
H	A	S	O	V	E	R		T	A	N				
B	U	T	T	E	D	I	N		T	E	N	D	T	O
O	D	I	E		B	L	A	C	K	W	I	D	O	W
M	I	L	L		A	L	G	A	E		K	A	N	E
B	O	L	L		G	E	S	T	S		E	Y	E	S

ANSWERS

Vivid Phrases (pages 164–165)

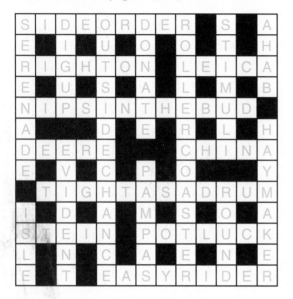

Fast Food, Hasty Reading (pages 168–169)

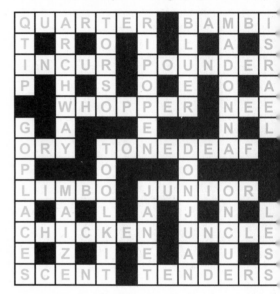

How Much Is There? (pages 166–167)

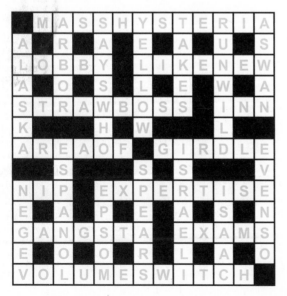

Ode to a Grecian -Ern (pages 170–171)

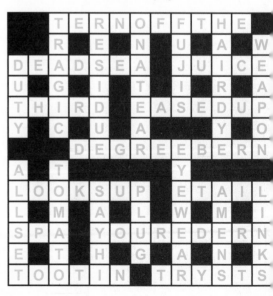